401(k)nowhow™
An Insider's Guide to Retirement Plan Options

Brian D. Heckert, CLU®, ChFC®, AIF®

Financial Solutions Midwest, LLC.

Financial Solutions From Trusted Advisors

ISBN-13: 978-0692788684

ISBN-10: 0692788689

Praise for *401(k)nowhow*™

Ted Benna, "Father of the 401(k)"
401(k) Benna, LLC
Newton, Pennsylvania
Brian's book will be a very useful tool for any 401(k) participant. Following the advice Brian gives will help new 401(k) participants make better decisions, substantially improving their prospects of retiring successfully. Brian also provides lots of specific advice to help those who are either near or in the early stage of retirement to make sound decisions that will increase the potential of keeping their income streams flowing during their retirement years.

H. Larry Fortenberry, CPA, CLU, ChFC
Executive Planning Group
Jackson, Mississippi
This book is a great resource for employees and plan sponsors alike. Brian's writing style will help the reader understand a very complex subject in a format that allows for easy reading. The chapters offer the ability to go directly to the subject and question at hand. His expertise also provides even the most sophisticated reader lessons on topics related to the 401(k) plan design.

Jennifer Borislow, CLU
Borislow Insurance Services
Methuen, Massachusetts
As you look toward retirement, ask yourself how much income you will need and how long will your savings last. Brian Heckert, an expert in the retirement planning field, outlines in this book a complete step-by-step guide for securing a successful retirement. It is a wonderful road map designed to help financial advisors, retirement plan professionals, and employers with the knowledge and expertise to guide participants toward achieving financial freedom.

Bryan Sweet, CLU, ChFC
Sweet Financial Services, Inc.
Fairmont, Minnesota
Building meaningful relationships with your employees is key to success in our highly competitive world for top talent. Having the right road map to making your 401(k) stand out and understood is key. Brian is a foremost expert on this subject and provides the needed tools and tips to streamline that process.

John Moshides, CLU, ChFC
Moshides Financial Group
Amherst, New York
Financial Solutions Midwest led by Brian Heckert has been a leading 401(k) expert for many years. Not only is he on the cutting edge of plan design issues, he has the knowledge and compassion required to help plan participants utilize their plan properly to allow for a meaningful retirement...that is where the rubber hits the road for companies that sponsor plans!

Ron Greenberg, CLU, AEP®
Greenberg & Rapp Financial Group, Inc.
East Hanover, New Jersey
Brian Heckert and his team have invested their energy and passion into becoming true experts in the retirement plan market. Their combination of industry knowledge with a thirst to be the best has been their blueprint and has led to recognition as a true expert in the field. However, not everyone can channel their expertise into a book that communicates the complex in a straightforward manner. Brian has managed to do exactly that!

Michael McNeil, MBA, CLU
Northwestern Mutual
Fairfield, Connecticut
This book by Brian Heckert is one of the best resources for anyone seriously interested in understanding the 401(k) plan. For most people, this is the cornerstone of their retirement plan. Brian's work covers a wide range of important facts about the value of saving for retirement and provides a hands-on approach for readers to strengthen their retirement planning knowledge. Just an excellent book.

Peter D. Maller, MBA, CFP®, AEP®
Maller Wealth Advisors, Inc.
Hunt Valley, Maryland
Brian has found a way to articulate the complex world of retirement planning into a script that is easy to read and comprehend. His many years of living in this Retirement Plan world and investing hugely along the way to "become the best" at his task is reason enough to read his book and "take in" what he has learned, and taught, over the decades!

Steven Plewes, CLU, ChFC, AIF®
Advisors Financial Strategies, Inc.
Germantown, Maryland
Just like everything that Brian Heckert takes on, this book is well thought out, thoroughly researched, and covers all the bases for employees and employers regarding how to optimize their 401(k) plans. His expertise and wisdom in this field, gained from decades of experience and focus, shine through. Taking

the time to read this book will be time well spent for benefit plan sponsors and participants in a 401(k) plan.

Jeffrey Cullen
Strategic Retirement Partners
Shorewood, Illinois

Brian brings a unique perspective that can come only with the experience of being involved with retirement plans from every angle during this transformative period in the industry: as a TPA (designing and administering plans), investment consultant (consulting plan sponsors and business owners), financial planner (working with participants), business owner, participant, and industry advocate (working on the government policy side). He has spent many years "getting his hands dirty," working directly with and counseling participants through the decision-making process. Many employers wonder what their employees are thinking. Brian knows. Their fears and anxiety surrounding these choices are acknowledged here and addressed with real-world solutions and useful information. The "Key Points to Remember" section at the end of each chapter provides a practical, easily digestible summary that allows the reader to move forward with actionable information. This book is a wonderful complement to any participant education program and is a valuable read for plan sponsors and plan administrators as well.

Dedication

The art is not in making money, but in keeping it.
— Proverb

This book is dedicated to everyone who sacrifices to save a dime today so they can have a dollar in their future.

Table of Contents

About the Author

Brian D. Heckert, CLU, ChFC, AIF, of Nashville, Illinois, is president of Financial Solutions Midwest LLC, an independent financial services practice. Through his unique service called 401(K)nowhow™, he meets one-on-one with employees who work for the corporate clients who participate in his 401(k) plans to ensure that every employee is getting the optimum benefit from his or her 401(k) plan.

In 2015, he served as president of the Million Dollar Round Table (MDRT) Executive Committee. He has consistently qualified for the highest levels of membership based on professionalism, dedication to ethical service, and volume of service his firm provides to its clientele.

Brian's Round Table volunteerism includes speaking at the MDRT Annual Meeting and MDRT Experience meeting, as well as service on multiple MDRT committees and task forces. Highlighted leadership roles include three years of service on the MDRT Foundation Board of Trustees and three appointments as Divisional Vice President: Membership and Leadership (2012), Annual Meeting Program Development Committee (2010), and Annual Meeting Program General Arrangements (2000).

He is a frequent industry speaker and has been quoted in numerous business, industry, and association publications.

Brian began working with 401(k) plans when he was twenty-one years old, in 1985. In 1998, he purchased a share in the company he had been working with for fourteen years. In 2001, he purchased the entire company. He began running the administration company on his own in 2001. At one time, his company serviced about 260 plans throughout the United States. He had approximately eight thousand employees covered under those plans, which totaled $350 million in assets.

In 2012, he sold the administration company, but he still maintains a relationship with about forty companies that have retirement plans. Today, his focus is on spending quality time with each of the 401(k) plan participants instead of working with employers on administration issues. He spends most of his time on plan design and employee education.

Brian works with six team members in three office locations: Nashville, Illinois; Carlinville, Illinois; Springfield, Illinois; and Janesville, Wisconsin.

Financial Solutions Midwest, LLC.

Financial Solutions From Trusted Advisors

Foreword

Retirement is a remarkable time in everyone's life to pursue their dreams and passions. During our working years, the most valuable asset we hold is our time. In retirement, there is an abundance of time. Are you going to pursue your passions or let your financial situation control your decision making?

For many people embarking on the golden years, there is some amount of worry and stress—have I saved enough money? Will I run out of money? What happens if I get sick? They wonder if they have planned properly. As an economist and author for more than twenty-five years, I have been witness to the retirement challenges that Americans are facing. Overwhelmed Baby Boomers do not know where to turn for advice. Financial advisors are also facing a challenging journey ahead with their clients as we move forward into an unknown economic future with new regulations.

Fortunately, Brian Heckert has penned a book that will help Boomers but also Millennials and Generation X and Y with their retirement journey. While most of this book is about the accumulation phase of retirement, Brian adds many valuable nuggets for those in retirement as well. Read carefully as Brian tells you more about the 401(k) plan than you ever knew existed! He is a true expert in this field.

Growing up in Glenwood, Minnesota, I was raised by my two parents who were school teachers. One common thing with retirement planning in that day was that they both had a pension. When discussing retirement, they would talk in terms of "We are ready to retire since we have $3,000 a month in income." Or "With Social Security and our pension, we have enough income to last for the rest of our lives." Fast forward to today's landscape, and the conversation has changed dramatically. A lot of people do not have a pension or an employee-sponsored retirement plan. Everyone is focused on obtaining a certain number; they just aren't sure how to get there. Back in the day, you were able to have a company-supported retirement plan, and Social Security provided a decent income as well. Today, we face a stressful do-it yourself retirement plan that cannot rely on Social Security alone.

The Defined Benefit Plan (DBP) provided by many companies has been replaced by the Defined Contribution Plan (DCP), such as a 401(k). These 401(k)s are now the most significant vessel for Baby Boomers and younger generations saving for retirement. It's now more important than ever to realize the intricacies of optimizing your retirement plan, especially 401(k)s. The 401(k) is a powerful investment vehicle that can help provide financial well-being for many years in the future.

I originally met Brian through Million Dollar Round Table (MDRT) when I was auditioning for a speaker's slot at MDRT's Top of the Table meeting. The audition was in Chicago, and it was really a nerve-racking time for me. Brian took me aside and shared with me some tips and took a real interest in helping me. In the years since, I have seen that caring side of him over and over again. He was someone who was widely respected among our community and was known specifically for his in-depth knowledge of 401(k)s. As I got to know Brian better, it was very blatant that he had an intensely passionate drive to help his clients retire properly. When I first read this book, I felt Brian's passion on every page. Brian and I both are on a mission to help 78 million Baby Boomers retire optimally. Brian's attention to detail about 401(k)s makes this book a must-read for financial advisors and clients alike who want to improve their knowledge immediately.

He reached the pinnacle of the insurance industry by becoming the president of the MDRT. This is arguably the most sought-after and prestigious position in the entire industry. He did that while still running a top insurance and investment practice in Illinois and Wisconsin.

Although this book may not solve every retirement problem you can face, it is an ideal step forward. Brian will take you deep into the world of 401(k)s: what they are, how they work, what to take advantage of, what to be careful of, how loans work, what types of investment strategies work best, the importance of self-discipline, and so much more!

Rather than leave retirement planning to chance, this book can provide real-world solutions to help you take action the moment you finish. I hope you enjoy Brian's meticulous and practical retirement solutions as much as I have.

Tom Hegna, CLU, ChFC, CASL
Economist, Author, and Speaker

Preface

Through my service called 401(k)nowhow™, my team and I provide one-on-one consultations with the employees who work for the clients in my 401(k) plans. In conducting more than five thousand of these meetings with employees, I have seen a recurring theme in every single one of them: People just don't understand how they can put enough money into their plan so they can retire comfortably. I have been around long enough to see success stories as well as stories of dismal failure. The factors that cause the successes are predictable, as are the factors that cause the failures.

In this book, I reveal what I have learned in more than thirty years of working with 401(k) plans—tips for optimizing your returns as well as common mistakes to avoid. I hope you will use this book to discover how you can be one of the success stories.

I have found that what is missing from most 401(k) programs is one-on-one attention for all participants. A typical scenario is that a large company will have an open-enrollment period for its benefits. The HR manager will invite a representative from the 401(k) company to speak to all employees for an hour. People are expected to learn in one hour a complex, complicated subject that will affect their ability to retire comfortably! Virtually all 401(k) administration companies fail to provide their plan participants with one-on-one consultations to ensure that they understand how the plan works, how they can get the most out of it, and how to adjust the plan based on major life events. Although the web-based technology is available in even the most basic plan offerings, few employees have the time or patience to go through the steps needed to determine proper investment allocations or contribution rates.

I believe it is a travesty that we expect millions of American workers to make decisions about their 401(k) plan that will affect their financial well-being for the rest of their lives after hearing only a cursory one-hour overview. The purpose of this book is to educate people about how to get the most of their plan. Spending a little time now to learn the do's and don'ts of 401(k) plans can pay huge dividends later. Mistakes are costly. Doing it right will allow you to retire comfortably and, most importantly, independently, on your terms.

Please note that paragraphs that are indented from the left margin and presented in bold type are legal disclaimers required by regulation.

Acknowledgments

A book project is a small project to start but a huge project to finish. This was accomplished with the help of many hands and the support of many people.

First is my wife Mary, who patiently watched the proofing process as we traveled around the world.

To my four children for giving me great input from a generation that is more attuned to saving for retirement than any other.

To my staff, Kathi and Brittany, for help with compliance, drafts, finding the most recent version, and keeping the process moving forward.

To my partner, Leo, for his input and assistance so I could find the time to write.

To my study group members Bryan, John, Ron, and Peter for their unending giving and growing ways.

To Libbye Morris for her help in in assembling and clarifying my thoughts.

To my broker dealer, Kestra Financial, and the wonderful staff who have guided me through the compliance maze.

And finally, to my many businesses that deal with their 401(k) issues daily and provide me with an opportunity to help their employees retire with dignity.

Introduction

We have a retirement-savings crisis in the United States. According to the many headlines and articles published every day, people are not saving for retirement. Yet, they are living longer than ever before, which means people need more money after retirement than they have at any time in history.

A 2013 report by the National Institute on Retirement Security paints a dismal picture of the retirement-savings status of American workers. Forty-five percent of working-age American households (38.3 million) have no retirement savings. Of those who do have retirement accounts, the typical working-age household has only $40,000 in retirement-account assets, and the typical near-retirement household has only $100,000. The report also reveals that access to retirement plans is at the lowest level since 1979, with only half of private-sector employees having access to workplace retirement benefits. The report concludes, "With limited retirement-plan access and minimal retirement savings, the majority of American households will not be able to maintain their standard of living after retirement, even if they work until age sixty-seven." [1]

Our mission at Financial Solutions Midwest is to help people understand retirement-savings plans, contribute to them, and leave the money in their accounts for as long as possible. Our proprietary service, 401 Edu(k)tion™, has helped thousands of employees receive an honest look into their current retirement plans to see if they match their dreams and goals. I hope this book helps you understand the critical role that a retirement-savings account like a 401(k) plan has in your financial future.

---

1 "The Retirement Savings Crisis: Is It Worse Than We Think?" Webinar presentation, National Institute on Retirement Security website, June 20, 2013, http://www.nirsonline.org/storage/nirs/documents/Retirement%20Savings%20Crisis/final_6-20_media_and_interested_parties_retirement_savings_crisis.pdf.

What Is a 401(k) Plan?

The assumption is that if you are reading this book, you already know what a 401(k) plan is; after all, this type of plan has been around since 1978—for more than thirty-five years. Here is the simple explanation: Put money in, invest the money, and pull the money out at retirement. If only it were that simple. Or is it?

Employees can put money aside for retirement in a 401(k) account using pre-tax dollars, which reduces taxable income. They will not be charged federal tax on the money until it is used during retirement. In most cases, employers match a portion of their employees' contributions. Because you receive tax advantages from setting aside money in a 401(k) plan, you may be limited to a maximum pre-tax contribution each year. In 2016, that deferral amount is $18,000, but you can contribute an additional $6,000, or $24,000, if you are age fifty or older. If your employer contributes to your plan, the total contributions from both of you cannot exceed $53,000 (in 2016).

Employers set aside employee contributions in a special account where the funds are invested in various options made available in the plan.

The bottom line is, the more you put away, and the earlier you begin doing it, the more money you can have when you retire.

The more you put away, and the earlier you begin doing it, the more money you can have when you retire.

Unfortunately, 401(k) plans have become complex. Only the most savvy investors are typically confident about getting the most out of a 401(k) plan. It may be unreasonable to expect the average American employee to understand how to optimize his or her return in the plan. But it's critical that you do. Understanding how your 401(k) plan works can help you accumulate enough financial resources to not only live on when you retire and are no longer earning a paycheck, but to live well. The decisions you make now regarding your 401(k) plan can affect your financial well-being for the rest of your life. People live longer today than they ever have, so it's not uncommon to be retired for thirty or forty years. Mistakes with 401(k) plans are common, costly, and can impact your retirement forever. With a little 401(k)nowhow™, we may be able to help you make decisions that will allow you to optimize your 401(k) plan so that you can save the most money possible for your retirement.

With a 401(k), the burden lies on employees to decide three key points:

1. How much of their income to put aside for retirement
2. What types of funds to invest in
3. How to turn that lump sum of money into a lifetime of income in retirement

It can be confusing, especially because the tax laws and the investment markets are constantly changing. Whether you are an employer or an employee, knowledge is power—and money.

Here are some statistics about 401(k) plans:

- According to the US Department of Labor, there are 638,390 defined contribution retirement plans in the United States; of those, 513,000 are 401(k) plans. They cover more than 88 million participants, and 73 million of them are active participants. [2]

- Nearly 80 percent of all full-time workers have access to employer-sponsored retirement plans, and more than 80 percent of them participate in a plan. At companies with five hundred or more workers, 89 percent have access to employer-sponsored retirement plans, and 90 percent of those employees participate. [3]

- Participants are saving an average of 6.8 percent of their pay. Employer contribution averages 4.5 percent of pay, up from 3.7 percent in 2010. [4]

- Assets from defined contribution plans like 401(k) plans represent 25 percent of the total retirement market and almost one-tenth of the aggregate financial assets of US households, as of the end of the third quarter of 2013. [5] (This same report says that in the first three quarters of 2013, 9.2 percent of defined contribution plan participants changed the asset allocation of their account balances, while 6.8 percent changed the asset allocation of their contributions.)

How the Plan Got Its Name

The IRS tax code is composed of a multitude of different provisions that define what a qualified retirement plan can and cannot do, as well as what people

---

2 "Private Pension Plan Bulletin," US Department of Labor, Employee Benefits Security Administration, June 2013, http://www.dol.gov/ebsa/pdf/2011pensionplanbulletin.pdf.

3 "Employee Benefits in the United States—March 2013," Bureau of Labor Statistics, US Department of Labor, press release, July 17, 2013, http://www.bls.gov/news.release/pdf/ebs2.pdf.

4 "401(k) Plans Are Working," Plan Sponsor Council of America website, October 17, 2013, http://www.psca.org/401-k-plans-are-working.

5 "Defined Contribution Plan Participants' Activities, First Three Quarters of 2013," research report on Investment Company Institute website, February 2014, http://www.ici.org/pdf/ppr_13_rec_survey_q3.pdf.

can and cannot do with money they contribute to an employer-sponsored retirement savings plan.

A 401(k) plan is a tax-qualified retirement plan sponsored by for-profit, or private-sector, employers, and many not-for-profits as well. The term "401(k)" refers to section 401 of the Internal Revenue Service (IRS) tax code and subsection k. Although it sounds mysterious and sometimes confusing, the term "401(k)" is used to describe many different types of retirement plans. Section 401 of the IRS tax code describes most of the defined contribution or "profit-sharing" types of plans sponsored by for-profit corporations (private-sector employers), including qualified pension, profit-sharing, and stock bonus plans.

The remaining lettered subsections either put limitations on plans or address different variables in section 401.

Two Types of Tax-Qualified Retirement Plans

There are two types of tax-qualified retirement plans. The first is a *defined contribution plan*. With this type of plan, an employee, the employer, or both contribute funds to the employee's retirement. A 401(k) is a defined contribution plan.

The second type of retirement plan is a *defined benefit plan*. This is what is commonly referred to as a pension. These plans offer guaranteed automatic payouts in retirement based on a formula that usually takes into account an employee's salary and years of service. The longer you work and the more you make, the higher your automatic payouts will be. Many large employers offered pension plans during the first half of the twentieth century through the 1980s, when they became less popular. The federal government and many state and local agencies still offer them today.

Although some people lament that pensions are pretty much a thing of the past, a well-run 401(k) may have even more advantages. Let's compare the advantages of the two plans:

Pension Advantages:

1. **Guaranteed income**—As long as the pension plan remains intact, employees can receive income for life. Basically, they will not outlive their money.

2. **Little to no maintenance**—Employees are not required to do anything with this plan except participate. Someone else (usually the employer) chooses the investments, administers the accounts, and maintains them throughout the employee's life.

3. **Required employer contributions**—Employers are required to make minimum contributions or face stiff penalties.

4. **Guaranteed protection**—The Pension Benefit Guarantee Corporation (PBGC) provides an additional layer of security that is triggered when an underfunded pension plan is terminated.

401(k) Plan Advantages:

1. **Ownership**—The money contributed to a 401(k) plan is legally yours (at market value). You also receive a vested portion of the employer contributions.

2. **Portability**—With a 401(k), you are able to roll the account balance into another 401(k) plan or an Individual Retirement Account (IRA).

3. **Control**—With a 401(k), you decide your investment risk, not someone else. Also, you control how much to contribute above what your employer contributes, allowing you to increase your retirement savings. With a pension plan, the employer has a predetermined amount they must contribute, and you are not allowed to add to the plan. Controlling when you want to retire and how much income you want to withdraw is another huge benefit for a 401(k) that is not the case with a pension. Finally, a 401(k) plan allows you access on a daily basis to check how your funds are doing. You can log in to your account online and check on it at any time, which isn't always the case with a pension. Because pensions are controlled by the employer, employees are not allowed to review the investment selection.

4. **Voluntary participation**—Although it is not recommended, you can suspend your contributions to your 401(k) plan or change the deferral amounts. This is not an option with a pension.

5. **Loans**—Loan provisions in some plans allow you to borrow certain amounts against your 401(k) plan, which is not possible with a pension plan. Each employer decides whether to permit loans.

6. **Earlier access**—You may legally be able to access your 401(k) plan money without penalty by age $59\frac{1}{2}$ (or even earlier under certain considerations).

7. **IRA option**—You can roll your 401(k) into an IRA if you wish. If you switch jobs and decide not to keep your money in your old 401(k) plan, you have the option to convert it into an IRA.

8. **Employer match**—Employer contributions may help you out significantly. Employers are allowed to make generous contributions to employees' 401(k) plans.

9. **Benefits for heirs**—The pension system guarantees payment during your lifetime, but the income will stop after your death unless there is a provision for the spouse. Pension funds are never available for an inheritance. With a 401(k) or IRA, prudent savers can actually leave significant money to their heirs.

10. **Flexibility in tax management**—With a pension, once a payment is started, it is rarely possible to stop or defer it. But with a 401(k), you can delay withdrawals or take out only a portion of your investments to keep more of your money tax-deferred.

An Historical Viewpoint by Ted Benna: The Way It Was

There is a widely held perception today that we once had a wonderful private retirement system where all employees were given a guaranteed lifetime pension benefit. Defined benefit pension plans funded and managed by employers are the only type of plan that provides a guaranteed income for life. A myth that has been perpetuated is that all workers were once covered by pension plans where they were guaranteed an income for life at retirement. Some smaller employers had pension plans, but typically only employees of large companies, banks, insurance companies, and hospitals were offered pension benefits. Pension coverage never exceeded 50 percent of the workforce.

The next point that is missed in this myth is that pension benefits were very insecure prior to the passage of the Employee Retirement Income Security Act (ERISA) during 1974. Some pension plans required you to be thirty or even thirty-five years old before you could become a participant. Employees usually had to stay with the same employer until age fifty-five or sixty before they would earn a vested pension. An employee's entire benefit would be lost if he or she left the employer prior to the applicable date required to become vested. Some employers were known for finding ways to discharge employees as they were approaching this point.

Pension plan funding requirements were extremely loose prior to ERISA. A company could promise pension benefits without ever being required to pay the unfunded liability associated with those benefits. They were required to pay only the interest on this liability. Such an arrangement would be like paying only the interest on your home mortgage without every paying the amount borrowed. This resulted in grossly underfunded pension plans. Companies were permitted to walk away from their plans whenever they wished without any obligation to retirees and employees other than to use whatever plan assets were available to provide benefits. As a result, only 40 percent of the benefits earned could be provided for a plan that was only 40 percent funded. Numerous underfunded plans were terminated, resulting in huge benefit losses for both retirees and active employees.

The outrage became so great that Congress could no longer avoid the problem, so they passed ERISA in 1974. The primary purpose of ERISA was

In 1974, Congress enacted the Employee Retirement Income Security Act (ERISA) to help protect American workers from having their retirement funds misappropriated.

to make pension benefits more secure. Vesting was improved, funding requirements were tightened, and the Pension Benefit Guaranty Corporation was created to provide an additional layer of security when underfunded plans were terminated.

Smaller employers were more likely to offer employer-funded profit-sharing plans, but many didn't have any plan. As stated earlier, small employers were unlikely to offer pension benefits. Some employers had very generous profit-sharing plans with contributions in excess of 10 percent of pay, but such plans were the exception rather than the norm. Contributions in the 3 to 5 percent of pay range were much more common. As we know today, 3 to 5 percent of pay is not enough to provide an adequate level of retirement income.

Like many myths about the good old days, this one about a time when all workers received a guaranteed lifetime pension when they retired is a fantasy rather than reality. Myths and fairy tales about the good old days are okay, but they aren't a sound basis for making major decisions about our national retirement system.

401(k) Plans Were Simple in the Beginning

Many consider Ted Benna to be the father of the 401(k) plan. During the Carter Presidency in 1978, Congress passed an add-on to tax code section 401 and called the paragraph "k". This paragraph was added to resolve the future of cash or deferred, employer-funded profit-sharing plans. These plans, which became popular among banks, were funded by an employer's end-of-year profit-sharing contribution typically equal to one or two week's pay. Employees had to defer 50 percent of the contribution to be invested for retirement. They could take the other 50 percent as cash to be used however they wished, or to also defer this portion to be invested until retirement. Paragraph k introduced new rules for such plans.

Benna co-owned The Johnson Companies, a benefits consultancy in suburban Philadelphia. At that time, he was helping a bank revise its retirement program when he developed the idea of using this new code section to allow employees to contribute to their own retirement on a tax-favored basis and for the bank to add a pre-tax match as a further incentive to encourage employees to save more money for retirement. The bank turned him down because its attorney didn't want the bank to try something that had never been done before. The attorney's concern was justified because paragraph k didn't include any provision for employee pre-tax contributions or employer matching contributions.

The first 401(k) savings plan with pre-tax employee contributions and an employer match was implemented at The Johnson Companies effective

January 1, 1981, for its own employees. IRS issued an approval letter for this plan during the spring of 1981. The Johnson Companies began marketing 401(k) plans to other companies by successfully seeking press coverage for this new idea. A *New York Times* article about 401(k) featuring Benna finally got things rolling in a big way.

Benna has stated in interviews that he knew 401(k) would grow rapidly because large employers already had thrift plans where employees made after-tax contributions to receive an employer matching contribution. Benna was confident these employers would be very interested in adding a pre-tax employee contribution option once they realized this would be possible. A few large employers were willing to move ahead, but many waited until the IRS issued proposed regulations during the fall of 1981. These regulations supported linking pre-tax employee contributions and an employer match to code section 401(k). This affirmed that 401(k) savings plans like Benna designed would be permitted.

In a 2011 interview, Benna noted that the 401(k) started as a simple plan with a simple goal: allow employees to contribute to their own retirement. The early plans featured only two investment options: a guaranteed fund and an equity mutual fund or company stock. The number of investment options grew over the years due to pressure from participants for more choices. "Now this monster is out of control," Benna once said. "We went from two to three options, then to six, then to fifteen and beyond. It is far more than what most participants are able to deal with. And I am not convinced we have added value by getting more complicated."

Are We Better Off Now?

There is strong evidence that employees are better off at this point due to 401(k) than without it. The first group of employees to consider are those who work for large employers. Most of these employers offered thrift plans in addition to a defined benefit pension plan. Employees made after-tax contributions to these thrift plans and received an employer match; however, these plans were generally nothing more than glorified Christmas clubs. Employees were permitted to take out their contributions at the end of each year; and, with most plans, they were also permitted to withdraw all the employer contributions after two years. It was common for more than 90 percent of employees to withdraw all their contributions and the employer contributions as soon as they could do so.

Large companies with these thrift plans already in place added a pre-tax employee deferral option soon after they heard this was possible. This new option forced employees to make a decision: either continue making pre-tax contributions that could be withdrawn at any time or start making pre-tax contributions that

I do not believe 401(k) plan makes the average worker more prepared for retirement.

could be withdrawn only prior to retirement for a financial hardship. Many employees decided to go with the pre-tax option, thereby becoming long-term rather than short-term savers. As a result, employees who did so accumulated substantial 401(k) balances by the time they retired. Social Security, the company pension, plus 401(k) savings have enabled these employees to achieve a higher level of financial security than would have been possible without 401(k).

The next group that benefited from 401(k) are employees who worked for smaller employers that offered a profit-sharing plan. These employers all added pre-tax employee contributions to their plans within a few years after 401(k) hit the market. The revised plans usually included pre-tax employee contributions, an employer matching contribution, and a profit-sharing contribution. The opportunity to make pre-tax contributions enabled these employees to build much larger account balances during the past thirty-five years than would have been possible with just employer profit-sharing contributions.

There are also hundreds of thousands of small employers that have adopted 401(k) plans during the past thirty-five years. Many of these employers would have either adopted solely employer-funded profit-sharing plans, or they wouldn't have adopted any retirement plan. These employees are also generally better off with 401(k) than would have been without it.

It is probably worth noting at this point that the Reagan Administration attempted to eliminate 401(k) during the mid-1980s. This attempt failed due to a very substantial lobbing effort by 401(k) participants urging members of Congress to retain 401(k). This effort helped to preserve 401(k); however, the maximum employee pre-tax contribution limit was reduced from $30,000 to $7,500 when President Reagan's Tax Reform Act was enacted.

The number of defined benefit plans (except for tax-driven plans maintained by professionals) has been on the decline since ERISA was enacted. One of the reasons is connected to the way PBGC works. ERISA gave PBGC the right to claim up to 20 percent of corporate assets when an employer terminates an underfunded pension plan. Accountants and other professional advisers warned businesses that didn't have a defined benefit plan not to adopt one after this fact became known.

ERISA also put in place maximum limits on the amount of pension benefit an employee of a company could receive. Up to this point, the financial well-being of senior executives was tied to the same pension plan and savings plan as all other employees. That linkage began to change to a point where non-qualified retirement plans known as SERPS and stock options became the major way for senior executives to build wealth. The benefits they could receive from their employer's pension plan and 401(k) became less and less important over the years.

The accounting profession also badly hurt defined benefit plans by changing the accounting rules, making a company's pension expense as reported to shareholders very unpredictable. The ERISA benefit limits and a change in accounting rules placed senior executives in a position where they could personally gain by eliminating the company's defined benefit pension plan. The expense reportable to shareholders is totally predictable with a defined contribution plan. Therefore, it is to senior management's benefit to have such plans rather than defined benefit pension plans. Having a predictable expense helps drive up the company's stock value, increasing the potential for a big payoff via stock options.

Concluding this section, the world for future workers is very different than what it was years ago. Very few employees in the private sector today are earning pension benefits. Most defined benefit plans that are still in existence are closed to new entrants, and most no longer allow employees to earn additional benefits. Newly hired employees are instead building savings for retirement in defined contribution plans where they have sole responsibility for getting it right. The rest of this book contains information that will help these employees achieve a successful retirement.

How Much to Contribute to Your Plan

The question employees ask me most often is, "How much do I need to contribute so that I can retire comfortably?"

In response, I jokingly respond, "How long are you going to live after retirement? Tell me how long you will need the money, and I will tell you how much you need to contribute." The Social Security Administration provides a life expectancy calculator on its website that will tell you how long you can be expected to live, based on average life spans, given your current age and your gender. Go to http://www.socialsecurity.gov/cgi-bin/longevity.cgi, enter your information, and the calculator will tell you the average life expectancy for someone your age. In addition, it will illustrate the life expectancy for people who are already sixty-two, sixty-seven, or seventy. For example, a woman who is now age fifty-three can expect to live about thirty-three more years. According to the calculator, by the time she turns sixty-two, she can expect to live another twenty-five years. That means that if she plans to retire at age sixty-two, she will need a plan to make her money last as long as she does.

True financial independence in retirement requires about twice the amount most employees will receive from Social Security.

Employees at different ages will need to contribute different amounts if they are to achieve what I consider a retirement income sufficient to allow them to remain "independent." It is usually not possible to achieve independence on Social Security alone. True financial independence in retirement requires about twice the amount most employees will receive from Social Security. If someone makes $1,500 a month from Social Security, then to maintain independence, she will need another $1,500 to $2,000 a month just to remain independent and avoid having to live with her adult children when she retires or live a substantially diminished lifestyle. To do that, which requires her to generate $20,000 a year of income, she will need a lump sum of at least $400,000 when she retires.

Three Life Stages

We can categorize 401(k) participants' lives into three general stages: wide-eyed enthusiasm, middle-aged malaise, and pre-retirement anxiety. The way you manage your 401(k) account often differs according to which life stage you are in:

If you are an employee in this age range	Minimum percent of your income we recommend that you contribute to your 401(k) plan
Age 30 or younger (wide-eyed enthusiasm)	At least 10 percent
Between 30 and 40 (middle-aged malaise)	At least 12 percent
Between 40 and 50 (pre-retirement anxiety)	At least 15 percent

The younger you are when you start contributing to your 401(k) plan, the more time your money has to grow.

See the chart titled "Are You on Target to Retire?" in the Appendix to find out how much you need to save to achieve your desired monthly income for thirty years.

The Magic of Compounding Interest

Albert Einstein said, "Compound interest is the eighth wonder of the world. He who understands it earns it...he who doesn't...pays it." That sums it up well.

When speaking with employees about the importance of an age-appropriate investment allocation, I often use what is called "the rule of 72" extensively to explain how to estimate the growth of money. It has to do with the power of compounding interest. The rule was discovered by mathematicians when they were looking for a way to estimate how long it would take something to double at a set rate of return. They found that the number 72 worked best at lower interest rates through about 15 percent, and 69 was the number that worked best at higher interest rates.

So, to estimate the number of years required to double an original investment, just divide the rate of return into 72. For example, let's say you invested $100 with compounding interest at a rate of 9 percent per annum. According to the rule of 72, 72 divided by 9 equals 8 years. Therefore, 8 years would be required for the investment to double and be worth $200 if it earned a 9 percent return.

Because many of the participants I meet do not consider compounding of returns and math in general to be their favorite topic, I try to use easy-to-understand examples and stories to help illustrate concepts relating to the growth of money and the importance of investing. An age-old story I often use might also help illustrate the power of compounding. It shows how a small investment made over a long period of time results in much more wealth than saving a lot of money in a short period of time.

According to one version of the story, an emperor of China was so excited about the game of chess that he offered the inventor of the game one wish. The inventor declared that all he wanted was one grain of rice on the first square of the chess board, then two grains on the second square, four on the third, simply doubling the number of grains of rice on each square and so on, through the 64th square. The unwitting emperor agreed to the modest request. He did not realize that it would result in a number of grains equal to 2 to the 64th power, which is 18 million trillion grains of rice—more than enough to cover the entire surface of the earth. The emperor, realizing that he had been duped, had the inventor of the game beheaded. Although it is not possible to double the investment returns of a 401(k) plan like in this example, it illustrates how powerful a tool compounding can be.

But illustrating the effect of compounding still works with money. The next story may hit closer to home for most participants. Let's say two twenty-year-old twin brothers start working for the same company at the same time. One puts $2,000 a year in his 401(k) plan for ten years at 6 percent interest and never puts in another dime after his thirtieth birthday. His twin brother goes out and buys a four-wheeler the first year, then a motorcycle, plays around with his money, doesn't put any aside, and thinks he has all the time in the world. On his thirtieth birthday, he makes his first $2,000 contribution to his 401(k) plan and continues contributing $2,000 each year for the next thirty-five years. After putting money aside for only ten years, the first brother, who invested a total of only $20,000, will have approximately 30 percent more money at age sixty-five than the second brother, who put in $2,000 a year for thirty-five consecutive years (a total of $70,000). Again, the moral of the story is, the earlier you begin saving, the more time your money has to grow.

Here is another example. Let's say a thirty-year-old has $10,000 in her account and doesn't want any risk. She just wants to keep it safe. Her money earns 3 percent interest and will double every twenty-four years. So, at age fifty-four, it would be worth $20,000, and it would not double to $40,000 until she turned seventy-eight. But if she would just take a little bit of investment strategy risk and possibly average 8 percent

Taking less risk can actually be the riskiest approach for younger employees.

11

interest, her money could double every nine years. This would mean that when she is thirty-nine, it would be worth $20,000, at age forty-eight, it would be worth $40,000, at age fifty-six, it would be worth $80,000, at age sixty-four, it would be worth $160,000, at age seventy-two, it would be worth $320,000, and by the age of seventy-eight, it would be worth more than $500,000. That's more than ten times the value of taking a lower risk. I have argued that sometimes, taking less risk can actually be the riskiest approach for younger employees! The approach I recommend for younger employees is to start early, take a little risk, and invest consistently for as long as possible.

Have You Checked Your Federal Income Tax Withholding Lately?

Compounding works like magic for younger people, but it doesn't make as much sense for a fifty-year-old because he has only about fifteen years left to put away money and for his money to grow. How can that fifty-year-old accrue enough to live on in retirement with such a short period of time to invest? I have worked with many older employees over the years who have gotten themselves into a trap—they spent a lot of money when they were younger, borrowed heavily, and now have no money left over to save. The common advice many have been told is simply, "See if you can find a percent or two here or there and do your best to save something." I always take it a step further by actually reviewing the employees' paychecks with them to try to find out the reasons they are not saving.

401(k)nowhow™ is the process we developed to help our clients get the most retirement savings out of their paychecks by reviewing their payroll deductions and their income tax deferral amounts. We look at an employee's total paycheck to verify all of the deductions, such as life insurance, other insurance deductions, and federal income tax withholding, making sure they are necessary. Because many employees set up these deductions to come out of their paychecks over a period of years and rarely change their income tax withholding amount, their paychecks become loaded with deductions that may not be relevant or necessary for their current needs. This review can often turn up 5, 10, or even 15 percent of an employee's paycheck to redirect toward his or her retirement by allocating it toward the 401(k). So that same employee who felt he could not afford to save any additional money is now able to save a significant amount without any change to his take-home pay. All of the additional savings come from the unneeded deductions or are redirected from a large income tax refund that is often spent unwisely. Using this technique, that fifty-year-old can now start the savings needed to get him closer to his retirement goal.

In almost 60 percent of cases, we find a common problem that is preventing people from saving: an excessive income tax withholding causing an excessive income tax refund check.

Let's say I'm talking with a fifty-year-old employee who makes $30,000 a year. She is saving just 3 percent toward retirement, or $900, but should be saving at least 15 percent of her salary, which is $4,500 a year, to come close to her retirement income goal. During our Edu(k)tion™ meetings, one of the first questions I will ask is if she receives an income tax refund check each year. We find that many people like her are often receiving as much as a $3,000 per year in an income tax refund. Let's do the math: $3,000 is 10 percent of $30,000, and $3,000 equals about $60 per paycheck. Each paycheck, she is short by about $60 because she is having $60 too much withheld from each paycheck. What these people have done is back themselves into a corner by not looking at the amount they need to withhold for taxes, only to have it sent to the IRS and eventually be returned to them in a refund check.

In almost 60 percent of cases, we find a common problem that is preventing people from saving: an excessive income tax withholding causing an excessive income tax refund check.

Throughout the year, many in this predicament are also forced to use their credit cards to fund weekly spending needs, thereby running up their credit card debt, which often adds another 5 or 10 percent to their monthly expenses. Then they use their tax refund to pay off their credit card, and the debt/refund/lack of saving cycle starts all over again while leaving little, if anything, for the 401(k) plan.

It's a horrible cycle, and I see it time and time again. We use a program as part of our 401 Edu(k)tion™ service that plainly shows employees how to make the changes they need to make to get out of the cycle. Often I find that these employees didn't intend to have big refund checks; it just happens. They started at a company in their twenties or thirties, and they were not married, or maybe they were married and had one child. Then life happened and they got married or had another child and then another, and their deductions increased, causing their income tax refund checks to go up. Their weekly need for money has increased, but they become addicted to this tax-refund cycle. Rarely does anyone ever show them how to adjust their W-4 withholding with the Payroll Department each time they have a baby to change their payroll deductions and increase their weekly paycheck. And almost never do they see the impact of making a small change to their withholding on their W-4, which, in turn, could be redirected into the 401(k) plan and debt reduction.

Simply by spending ten or fifteen minutes with an employee during our 401 Edu(k)tion™ meetings on how to set up his W-4 withholding properly, we can often find another 7 to 10 percent of an employee's salary that can go into a 401(k) plan and possibly have enough left over to cover other bills. That will give him more weekly income in his take-home pay so that he can possibly start paying cash for expenses and pay down his credit card bills, putting an end to the debt/refund cycle!

The Power of Increasing Savings by Just 1 Percent More Every Six Months

We sometimes think that employees who make lower salaries are the only ones who have a difficult time saving money. But I see plenty of people who make $80,000 to $100,000 a year or more who are in the same type of situation. As their income goes up, their lifestyle demands go up, and they get themselves in the same debt trouble as those who make less money. Life encroaches on people's savings, so we focus on getting people into a stronger financial position incrementally.

We encourage regular meetings to show them how to contribute an extra 1 percent; 1 percent per week is about $6 for a $30,000 earner. Saving 10 percent increases your savings by $60. That is a big jump for a lot of people, often too big, so many people will not make a change. We encourage people to increase the amount of their contribution by 1 percent every six months. It's amazing how quickly they can make up for lost time and not even notice that $6 being deducted from each paycheck. If they continue this increase cycle of 1 percent every six months, they can get to that 10 percent savings rate in just five years. That seems like a long time, but many people will never reach it at all if they don't start with the first 1 percent.

It is unfortunate that more than one-third of Americans with 401(k) plans have never increased their 401(k) contribution rate. According to TIAA-CREF's "Investing in You" survey conducted in May 2014, 36 percent of Americans who contribute to an employer-sponsored retirement plan have never increased the percentage of their salary that they contribute to their company's plan. Another 26 percent of workers have not increased their contribution more than one year. And 57 percent of workers did not increase their plan contribution after their last raise. [6]

401(k)nowhow Investment MaXimizer™ Review

With our 401(k)nowhow Investment MaXimizer™ strategy, we help people optimize their after-tax returns. This strategy reviews the savings allocations of the 401(k) as well as their personal holdings. We will often allocate the most aggressive investments or their stock holdings to their personal portfolio outside of the 401(k) plan so that they can take advantage of all of the capital gains. We then allocate the conservative portions of their total portfolio inside of the 401(k) plan. We do this to shield the returns on these assets from ordinary income tax, which is taxed at a higher rate than dividends and capital gains.

The MaXimizer™ strategy allows an employee to keep the same investment allocation risk while using the tax rates on capital gains and dividends to increase the net returns. For someone with a large portfolio split between their 401(k) and a personal investment account, this could add significant tax

---

6 "TIAA-CREF Investing in You Survey," Executive Summary, TIAA-CREF website, August 12, 2014, https://www.tiaa-cref.org/public/pdf/C18501AugustInvestinginYouSurveyExecutiveSummary.pdf.

14

savings, which helps increase total yield.

A number of times over the years, we have worked with employees who have large portfolios with a balanced strategy, with approximately 50 percent conservative, in bonds, and 50 percent aggressive, in mostly dividend-paying stocks. Using the MaXimizer™ strategy, we would recommend allocating most of the conservative money ($500,000) inside the 401(k) plan, and we would invest the other $500,000 aggressively, in stocks and other capital-gains type of assets into the employee's personal account to save on income tax. Because the bonds are often taxed at ordinary income tax rates, placing them inside of the 401(k) plan would not add any additional income tax to the withdrawal. However, stocks placed inside of the 401(k) plan subject those gains to ordinary income tax when the employee could take advantage of the much lower capital gains and dividend rates. Also, if there is a need to raise cash for emergencies and the stock market investments are down in value, the employee could take a loan from the 401(k) plan to cover his short-term need.

The main benefit of this review is to help employees realize that maximizing the tax benefits of the different investments can also provide additional yield to a portfolio.

How to Read Your Account Balance Statement

A question we hear often from employees is, "How do I read my statement?" They receive quarterly statement mailings or possibly e-mails from their plan's administrator, and they can even access their 401(k) website daily. But the information can be overwhelming. We spend time with people teaching them how to read their statements and to know what to look for on a statement in just a matter of seconds.

Here is what to look for. All statements define a time frame, usually quarters or three months. They include the beginning balance, contributions made, investment earnings, and the ending balance. But what confuses participants most is all of the legal wording. Most of that information is there simply to add legal disclaimers or satisfy the regulators.

It is important to check your statement at least quarterly against your paycheck to make sure the contributions you are making are getting credited to your account. Look at how much you started with, how much you added, how much your money earned, and your ending balance.

Taking twenty seconds to review your statement every quarter may help you discover costly errors.

Check the withdrawal area to make sure no withdrawals were taken out of your account without your knowledge. You are allowed to withdraw money from your 401(k) account for certain types of hardship and sometimes for loans. It is rare, but from time to time, we see an incorrect Social Security number or a calculation error on a statement, so it is in your best interest to check it regularly.

Once you learn what to look for, it should take you only a few seconds to look at your statement and compare your contribution amount shown on your statement against the amount taken out of your paycheck. If that is correct, then move on to the amount of gain or loss, and you can rest for another three months! It is that simple.

Sometimes, not often, we hear of an employer who is not making contributions to an employee's account because the company is in financial trouble or just being lazy with payroll responsibilities. We also see situations in which contributions are not allocated to the correct account. That happens a bit more often due to payroll lapses or clerical errors. The more quickly you can catch an error, the sooner it can be corrected.

The standard IRS deadline for an employer to send the employee deferrals to the investment company is about seven to ten days maximum after they are withheld from an employee's paycheck. The time allowed is based on how quickly the employer settles other payroll-related deductions like federal income taxes.

It is also helpful to have a range in mind for what you consider to be an acceptable quarterly gain or loss. Your financial advisor can help you determine these amounts. Look at your investment return and see how it compares to the ranges you have in mind. However, always keep in mind that the markets can fluctuate significantly on a quarterly basis. This should be only the first step in the process of doing a thorough review.

Fear: A Costly Roadblock

Fear is a powerful deterrent and a costly roadblock to making wise investment decisions. When a lot of people hear that their 401(k) money might be invested in the "stock market," they immediately think of the friend or family member who lost large amounts of money in the stock market during the 2008 economic downturn or maybe in the Tech Crash of 2000.

While I was writing this book on an airplane, the person sitting in the seat next to me shared this exact same fear. He was a high-level manager for a major US corporation. Because he didn't understand how investments in a 401(k) plan work, he said, "Why don't I take that money and put it somewhere else or spend it and worry about saving it later?" It becomes an easy choice for people to make because they can see the money in their checking account and can access it today. They feel it's easier to do nothing, or do something familiar but unwise, than to contribute to a plan that will possibly reduce their take-home pay for the next thirty years and prevent them from accessing it for several decades. That just doesn't sound appealing to someone who does not fully understand how the process works.

In fact, a 2013 study revealed that investors are much more afraid of making a bad investment decision than they are of doing nothing and missing an opportunity. Research has shown that, of the investors in a study who made bad investment decisions, 92 percent regretted that decision and suffered feelings of "action regret." Only 8 percent who had the opportunity to choose an investment opportunity that did well, but chose not to invest, suffered "inaction regret." The fear of making a bad decision also leads plan participants to invest more conservatively than they should. As a result, they elect allocations in their 401(k) plan accounts that favor fixed-income investments over stocks. Because of the lower yields, they may never accumulate a balance large enough to meet their retirement goals. [7]

Many people fear losing everything. Education and exposure to success stories can help people make wiser choices.

Very few young people who meet with me want to retire at the age of seventy-two. Fewer still want to put money into a plan they don't understand. They are not uneducated people; they just have not been exposed to the long-term effect of saving in a retirement plan. They know they should invest, but they would rather have money in their pocket and make incorrect decisions on their own than to make a wrong choice with a plan they don't understand and lose everything. And that is what many people fear—losing everything. Education and exposure to success stories can help people make wiser choices. It is also what is needed to ensure that their money is working for them versus them working for their money!

Enhancing Education: 401 Edu(k)tion™

Many of the big investment firms and insurance companies have substantial 401(k) servicing departments. They will often send a retirement plan advisor out to a company for a regular investment education program. They often stand in the front of the room and talk to a large group of employees for forty-five minutes to an hour. They offer sophisticated and easy-to-use websites explaining retirement options for employees.

However, in my experience, it is often the rare case for the rep to sit down with individual employees and listen to their concerns, questions, and financial goals and ensure that the choices they make are appropriate for their age, family situation, level of income, and financial goals. Most advisors simply make sure the employee chooses the desired level of investment risk and signs the enrollment form in the correct spot. Maybe once a year, the advisor will send out an e-mail encouraging employees to log on to the investment website and review their investment mix. But employees rarely do that because they don't understand the implications of changing the level of risk or their investment mix. Most people haven't been exposed to 401(k) plans enough to know how they work, and no one, including the investment rep, has taken the time to educate them. Plus, the employer is prevented from giving advice due to federal regulations and liability concerns.

---

7 "Fear of Bad Investment Decisions Holds Back 401(k) Plan Participants," Employee Benefit News website, March 4, 2014, http://ebn.benefitnews.com/blog/ebviews/fear-of-bad-investment-decisions-holds-back-401k-plan-participants-2739649-1.h.

I realize that, economically, it is difficult to justify a service provider or independent rep giving one-on-one consultations to every employee. It is also not feasible for an employer to bring in an independent financial advisor for a fee to educate its employees on the plan investment options. That takes a lot of time and money, but it's the true service I think we should be providing as advisors. We are not doing our jobs as 401(k) professionals unless every employer and employee in our plan understands their options, the implications of their choices, and most of all, the consequences of not acting at all. This is why I developed the 401 Edu(k)tion™ service and why it has been so successful for the employers and employees who use it.

Chapter 1 Summary: Key Points to Remember

1. A 401(k) plan is a tax-qualified retirement plan sponsored by for-profit, or private-sector, employers, and many not-for profits as well.

2. The term "401(k)" refers to section 401 of the Internal Revenue Service (IRS) tax code and subsection k.

3. Employees can put money aside for a retirement in a 401(k) account using pre-tax dollars, which reduces taxable income. They will not be charged federal tax on the money until it is withdrawn.

4. The government sets limits on the amount you can contribute to a 401(k) plan. In 2016, that deferral amount is $18,000, but you can contribute an additional $6,000, or $24,000, if you are age fifty or older. If your employer contributes to your plan, the total contributions from both of you cannot exceed $53,000 (in 2016).

5. The more money you put away, and the earlier you begin doing it, the more money you will have when you retire.

6. In 1974, Congress enacted the Employee Retirement Income Security Act (ERISA) to help protect American workers from having their retirement funds misappropriated.

7. Although many people lament the fact that pension plans are becoming a thing of the past, 401(k) plans actually offer more advantages than pension plans, such as employer matching, voluntary participation, and the ability to transfer benefits to heirs.

How Does It Work?

In my almost thirty years of working with participants, it is a small percentage who truly understand the concept of deferring money from their paycheck today to receive a possible income ten, twenty, thirty, forty, or more years in the future. They watch their account balance go up or down, but they still often feel unsettled with the whole concept. The many rules and regulations that are enacted seemingly every year add another layer of confusion and distrust. And a major stock market correction like the one we witnessed in 2008–09 leaves an indelible impression that people's savings can drop substantially at any moment. That creates just the added amount of uncertainty many need to say, "Enough already! I don't want to participate, no matter how much you try to convince me it is in my best interest."

Let's take some time to address these concerns and give you a better understanding of the rules and terminology used with 401(k) plans.

A Shared Responsibility

Unlike pension plans, which are funded entirely by employers, 401(k) plans may be funded by both employers and employees. Employer contributions are considered "profit sharing." That was a term used in the past, when companies would make a profit and then contribute to employees' retirement as a percentage of that profit. Today, companies do not have to actually show a profit to make a contribution, so it is categorized as just an employer contribution. Because the employer is making the contribution on behalf of the employee, and it does a social good, the company is entitled to a tax deduction from the government for contributions it makes to employees' accounts.

The contribution from the employer can be made as a flat percentage of an employee's pay, a flat dollar amount, or a matching amount. The company's leadership could decide, for example, to contribute 10 percent of all employees' pay to the plan. Or they could decide to contribute $10,000 and divide that amount evenly among the participants as a percentage of their pay.

One of the most common types of employer contributions is a match percentage. With this option, the employer will make a contribution to an employee's 401(k) plan only if the employee contributes to the plan as well. Match formulas can be as varied as the companies that make the contributions. A company might contribute a dollar-for-dollar match, with a limit. An example might be that if the employee contributes 5 percent of pay, the company will match that with an additional 5 percent of pay contribution. That means the employee and employer would be contributing a total of 10 percent of the employee's pay to the plan. For example, if an employee earning

$30,000 contributes $1,500, the employer will contribute an additional $1,500. The company could set, say, a 5 percent limit so that no matter how much the employee contributes above 5 percent of pay, the employer portion will never be more than 5 percent of pay.

Another match formula could be a 50 percent match with a limit. For example, the employee contributes 4 percent of pay, and the employer makes a "50 percent match" for an additional 2 percent of pay—a total of 6 percent of pay between the two of them.

The employer's contributions are tax-deductible to the corporation and nontaxable to the employee until withdrawn. This means it is not added to the federal and state wage taxation for the employee, compliments of the US government. According to President Bush's 2009 budget, the tax exemption for employer plans was projected to cost the federal government $541.3 billion from 2009 through 2013. When IRAs and Keoghs were added, the tax revenue loss estimate was $690.71 billion for 2009–13. [8]

The biggest advantage of a 401(k) plan over other types of individual savings plans is that you get your tax break as you go, with each contribution.

Employee contributions are deducted from their paychecks before federal and state taxes (excluding Pennsylvania), but after Social Security taxes. Contributing to a 401(k) plan will not reduce your Social Security benefits. With a traditional 401(k) plan, the money you contribute to the plan is fully tax-deductible, and you get the immediate tax break with each paycheck. In contrast, contributing to another retirement option such as an individual retirement account (IRA) requires a contribution first, and then you claim the tax deduction later when you file your income tax return. The biggest advantage of a 401(k) plan over other types of individual savings plans is that you get your tax break as you go, with each contribution.

The most important thing to remember is that one of the biggest variations among employer 401(k) plans is the formula for the employer contributions and how they match, or the percentage they might contribute to the plan. The plans vary as much as the rules that govern them. However, the employee contributions are all limited by the government, and employees should not get confused by that amount. Today's limits are 100 percent of pay up to $18,000 for those under age fifty and $24,000 for those over the age of fifty. An employee making $15,000 per year could actually save her entire paycheck! While this seems unreasonable to defer all of your paycheck, we have employees doing this to catch up on their retirement savings and then living off of the other spouse's income. With this high limit, anyone should be able to contribute the necessary amount needed, no matter what the employer contributes on their behalf. Also note that many employers will match only if

8 "Tax Expenditures and Employee Benefits: Estimates from the FY 2009 Budget," Employee Benefit Research Institute (EBRI) Fact Sheet, February 2008.

you are actively contributing to the plan.

Many employers match only while a participant is actively contributing; therefore, it may be disadvantageous to front-end your contributions so that you have contributed all you plan to contribute before the year ends rather than contributing for the entire year. For example, assume your employer matches the first 6 percent of pay that you contribute and you earn $150,000. You set your contribution rate at 15 percent of pay because you have been told this is how much you should contribute. But you must stop contributing when you hit the $18,000 maximum. If your employer's 401(k) is like most plans, the matching contributions will stop at that point; therefore, you should check with your employer to see whether this is how the plan works. If so, plan your contributions so you are contributing at least 6 percent of pay for the entire plan year. In this instance, reducing your contribution rate to 12 percent will enable you to contribute $18,000 and get the full match. You may need to adjust your contribution rate each year as your pay and the maximum contribution allowed changes.

The Safe Harbor Rule

Numerous federal regulations govern 401(k) plans by encouraging broad participation and preventing owners and highly compensated employees (HCEs) from receiving disproportionately greater benefits than other employees. Plans must either satisfy a series of nondiscrimination tests each year or be designed to satisfy certain "safe harbor" standards that are not discriminatory. The basic purpose of a safe harbor designation for a plan is to provide rank-and-file employees with a fully vested contribution so that the HCEs can defer into the plan.

Before the government allowed for a safe harbor election, employers were forced to calculate the average deferral percentage by the non-HCEs each year to determine the maximum amount of deferral contribution that was allowed by the HCEs. This would often require a distribution of excess deferrals to the HCEs who violated the contribution limits. Because these calculations were often made well after April 15th, the personal income tax deadline, many HCEs would be forced to refile and reclaim these excess deferrals, causing major tax headaches. In recognition of this unfair burden, the industry and the government came up with a set of "safe harbor" guidelines that, if met, would pass the testing and allow HCEs to contribute the maximum without the need to return excess deferrals.

An employer can satisfy the contribution requirement by making either a nonelective contribution or a matching contribution on behalf of each eligible non-highly compensated employee (NHCE). The contribution can, but is not required to, be made on behalf of HCEs as well.

The nonelective contribution must be at least 3 percent of compensation for the plan year for each eligible employee, regardless of whether or not they make salary deferral contributions.

The matching option requires the employer to match plan participants' elective deferrals at the rate of 100 percent of the first 3 percent of compensation deferred, plus 50 percent of the next 2 percent of compensation deferred (a maximum match of 4 percent). There are other match combinations that can satisfy the safe harbor, but these are the most common.

Roth 401(k)s: Taxed Now…Tax-Free Later

The Roth 401(k) is another type of retirement savings plan. The US Congress authorized it under the Internal Revenue Code, section 402A. It represents a unique combination of features of the Roth IRA and a traditional 401(k) plan. Since January 1, 2006, US employers have been allowed to amend their 401(k) plan documents to allow employees to elect a Roth IRA-type tax treatment for a portion or all of their retirement plan contributions.

Most employers offer their employees a choice to defer into regular or Roth 401(k) plans. With a Roth plan, you pay the taxes now and get tax-free growth in the future. With a traditional 401(k), you take the tax deduction now, even if it means paying taxes later.

A Roth 401(k) allows you to contribute money into the plan after tax. When you do that, you give up the immediate tax deduction. But the real benefit is that (under the current IRS rules) you can receive the income from both your contribution and the growth, if any, free from federal income taxes.

So how do you know when it makes sense to select the Roth plan? It depends on what you think your tax bracket might be in during retirement and also if you will need access to lump sums for large purchases. It is also important to review your current income tax bracket. If a single employee is making less than $35,000 a year, she should almost exclusively contribute to Roth because she is paying very little, if anything, in true income taxes. She is in a low tax bracket and may even qualify for an Earned Income Tax Credit from the federal government. Employees who have incomes between $35,000 and $110,000, in my opinion, should be doing about 50/50—half in a Roth plan and half in a traditional 401(k) plan. It is difficult to predict if you will eventually be in a higher or lower tax bracket. But having a significant amount of money in Roth gives you the ability to make creative tax-planning decisions after you retire.

Let's say you have $100,000 in a Roth account, in addition to a significant amount of money in a traditional 401(k) plan. When you retire, you may need a lump sum of money for vacations or to buy a car. You could access the Roth money without having to worry about it impacting your federal income tax bracket in retirement. Under current rules, if you file your federal taxes as an individual and your combined income—defined as your adjusted gross income and nontaxable interest plus one-half of your Social Security benefits—is below $25,000, your benefits won't be taxed at all. If your income is between $25,000 and $34,000, up to 50 percent of your benefits may be subject to tax. For income of more than $34,000, up to 85 percent of your benefits may be considered taxable income.

A retiree who can live very comfortably at about $40,000 a year might need a new car, so he or she will have to withdraw $30,000 out of the 401(k) plan. By adding the $30,000 withdrawal to the $40,000 annual income, that total income is now $70,000. It will increase the tax rate significantly by withdrawing the $30,000. Not only will income be taxed on the $30,000; now the Social Security taxation rules significantly increase the tax impact on the all of the income.

You might consider a more aggressive investment strategy on the Roth portion of your plan than you do on your individual 401(k) portion.

Roth Investment Selection: Maximize the Tax Advantages

Because the Roth portion of your 401(k) plan is not currently subject to income taxes at retirement, you might consider a more aggressive investment strategy for the Roth portion of your plan account than you do on your regular 401(k) portion. I recommend using the Roth for the most aggressive investments in your portfolio to increase the growth potential. It makes sense to try to get the most return out of the Roth, which will then come out federal income tax-free!

This strategy is one that is often overlooked and can add significant tax advantages and yield to your retirement.

The Retirement Plan Comparison Grid in the Appendix shows a comparison of traditional and Roth 401(k) plans.

Investment Selections

In my work with employees, I find that their toughest decision after deciding how much to put in is to decide where to invest money. As I mentioned in the Introduction, in my opinion, it is a travesty that we, in this industry, give employees a thirty-five- to forty-five-minute talk once a year on their 401(k) plan and expect them to be able to understand and absorb the risk inherent in their own investment strategy. I have spent thirty years in this business and still have a tough time getting a handle on what is risky and what's not risky. Yet we offer employees only one meeting a year, and they have to determine their entire destiny based on that cursory overview. If they are wrong, they will pay a steep price because of their decisions.

Because many employees do not understand or feel qualified deciding where to invest their money, they often default to the most conservative option. They want to take very little risk when they are twenty-five or thirty years old because they don't want to lose their money. But by taking the conservative approach, they lose out on one of the greatest miracles of the financial world, which, as discussed earlier, is compound interest.

Let's say a twenty-five-year-old who makes $500 a week contributes 4 percent of her salary into the plan, and the company matches it dollar for dollar up to 4 percent of salary. Assume she gets a slight increase in her wages per year and earns a 5 percent return on her money. At age sixty-five, that employee would have $385,000. A portfolio with a 50/50 blend—50 percent of her money in a lower-risk investment and 50 percent in higher risk like a US stock portfolio—historically has produced a similar return over a forty-year period.

If that employee eliminated the lower-risk portion, invested all of her money in stocks, and was investing for a 9 percent annual rate of return, the same contributions would be worth more than $1 million. So a twenty-five-year-old who wants no risk has possibly just given up about $700,000 over that period of time. That's where I stress the importance of the advisor. We're in a strange environment right now in the 401(k) world. Regulators are clamping down on what advisors can do and the advice they can give. Yet it is a period of time when that twenty-five-year-old needs an advisor to work with her more than any time in history because of the risk of loss if she doesn't do it right.

What Is Risk?

If you are too conservative with your retirement account, you may run the risk of underfunding your retirement.

There are two major types of risk when it comes to investing: liquidity risk and market value risk. The stock market turmoil in 2008 and 2009 is vivid in people's minds. When people see the value of their accounts decrease on their statements, it terrifies them. But what they don't see is the erosion of growth they give up by saying, "I don't want any risk to my portfolio. Give me little risk, and I will just live off of what's there." By being too conservative, they often do not realize that they may be forfeiting hundreds of thousands of dollars in future growth potential, and they risk not having enough to retire comfortably.

Risk Is Relative

Choosing a more risky investment might be scary. But risk is relative. Let's look at an example of "relative risk." I might think that what a steel-plant worker does every day is dangerous and risky. Yet when he does his job, he is well aware of the risk of his job and how to minimize those risks he faces every day. He knows how to handle the risk. He knows where to walk in the steel plant and which areas to avoid so that he doesn't get scalded or possibly killed, whereas I am not familiar with the surroundings and may accidentally expose myself to harm if I attempt to do his job. Reverse that scenario. Now that steel-plant worker is in the company lunchroom during one of my 401(k) presentations, and I have to help him understand where not to invest and where to stay safe to avoid being seriously "hurt" in the stock market.

I know the pitfalls and have been exposed to the dangers. I have the experience in dealing with these investment "dangers," so I understand it. I have seen people take too much risk and lose a lot of money by trying to time the market in a decline. I have also seen people be too conservative and lose a lot of money due to a lack of return and erosion of principal due to inflation.

One of the hardest things I do is help people understand the different levels of risk. There is no benchmark to judge risk. How do you evaluate risk-adjusted returns? Few people have been trained in this area, and fewer still can explain it to the average 401(k) participant! But once you get the training and education, you learn how to accept the risk that allows your money to possibly experience the returns you need. Included in the Appendix is a popular "Investment Risk Assessment Profile" to help you better judge your personal risk tolerance.

A lot of people think risk is related to age or life stage. That is not true. Risk discussed in the context of age may often not be relevant at all. Look at it from this standpoint. Let's say a sixty-year-old woman has accumulated $300,000, but she is willing to work until she is seventy. She could possibly live for thirty or forty more years based on her family history, so she has to make her money last for thirty years after she retires. I don't look at age as much as I look at the ten years before somebody retires and the five years after they retire. We call those years the "retirement hot zone" because these are the fifteen most important years in a person's investment timeline. Mistakes in managing risk in those years could jeopardize the entire account and leave the retiree without enough money to live the lifestyle she desires. That fifteen-year period is when we need to monitor your risk level with utmost interest. That could be at age forty-five or at age sixty—whenever a person is going to retire. Because of inflation and the uncertainty down the road, you can't just turn off all risk, which a lot of people think they want to do when they reach retirement.

We call the ten years before retirement and the five years after retirement the "retirement hot zone" because they are the fifteen most important years in a person's investment timeline.

The five years before retirement are important because losses in those years would be hard to recover in such a short time. The next ten years are important because this is the time when the investment objective changes from accumulating to distributing. A portfolio that is distributing money for income is at risk because liquidating shares from a down market have a higher impact on long-term values.

Here is why. Let's say you have a stock priced at $10 per share and you own 10,000 shares for a total of $100,000. At this share price, you would need to liquidate only 500 shares, 5 percent of the shares owned, to equal a $5,000 distribution (500 shares x $10 = $5,000). Now, if the market goes down and the shares are only $5 per share, you would need to liquidate 1,000 shares to equal the same $5,000. This requires a 10 percent liquidation in the number of shares to equal the same $5,000. Two years in a row of this type of activity could devastate a portfolio very quickly if the amount of the distribution is not reduced or the market does not recover. During the "retirement hot zone," we attempt to reduce risks and volatility through the investment selection and managing the amount of the distributions from the most risky investments.

What Is the Difference between Investment Risk and Volatility?

Risk is exposure to the chance of injury or loss, a hazard or dangerous chance, and the degree of probability of such loss. If you are worried about the "risk level" of a certain investment, you are worried about the potential permanent loss of your money. [9]

Volatility refers to how much your 401(k) investments can go up or down based on the performance of the market. If you look at the share prices in any one of the stock indexes like the Dow Jones Industrial Average (DJIA) or the S&P 500, daily volatility is a reality. (The S&P 500 Index is an unmanaged group of securities considered to be representative of the stock market in general. You cannot directly invest in the index. The DJIA is a popular indicator of the stock market based on the average closing prices of thirty active US stocks representative of the overall economy.) You might see upswings of 1 to 2 percent in one day. You might also see little to no gain. Daily volatility has been as much as 1 to 2 percent, and one-year volatility has been as much as 10 to 30 percent, either up or down. But over a five-year period, the market generally becomes less volatile. The longer the period of time you analyze an investment, the less volatility you should see from start to finish.

For younger employees who have thirty to forty years until retirement, the daily volatility is less important because they often will not need access to the money for many years. However, daily and yearly volatility are more significant for those employees in the five to ten years before and after retirement because they will need to turn the account into an income stream by selling portions of their account during those years.

Wait and Watch

One of the most common mistakes people make with their 401(k) investments is reacting too quickly when they see movement in the market. Mixing emotions and money is often very dangerous to the performance of your account. In 2008 and 2009, when the stock market was down 20 to 30 percent or more, many participants made decisions to move their entire account balances out of the stock market into what they perceived to be safer

---

9 "The Difference between Risk and Volatility," Begin to Invest website, December 30, 2013, http://www.begintoinvest.com/difference-risk-volatility/.

investments. They got scared. It is this type of move that caused employees to permanently lose money in the market unless they were able to come back into the market after the biggest declines. Quite honestly, most investors were scared because we were seeing the entire market freeze up and the economy almost come to a halt. It was at this time that many participants joked that their 401(k) had become a 201(k)!

During that period, for example, a participant who had $100,000 and lost $20,000 and then decided to move the remaining $80,000 into an investment with no stock-market risk missed out on the rise in the markets that came the following years.

He permanently lost the eventual gain because he was afraid to get back into stocks. Many participants felt the same way and continued to watch the market increase, fearing another market decline and being frozen into thinking that if they came back into the market, they would face another decline. Now, almost eight years have passed since the 2008–09 decline, and we are still seeing some employees with their account balances in the most conservative investments, unwilling to face the prospect of another decline. But while waiting for the market to go down so they can get back in, they watch in agony as it has climbed back to pre-decline levels. Basically, they have been waiting to avoid another drop, only to miss out on a significant rally.

One of the most common mistakes people make with investments is reacting too quickly when they see movement in the market. Mixing emotions and money is often very dangerous to the performance of your account.

As of the first half of 2016, stocks have gone through another growth cycle, and participants are starting to invest aggressively again. According to a recent article on *The Wall Street Journal*'s website, retirement investors are putting more money into stocks than they have since markets were slammed by the financial crisis eight years ago. Stocks accounted for 67 percent of employees' new contributions into retirement portfolios in March 2014, according to recent data from Aon Hewitt, which tracks 401(k) data for 1.3 million people at large corporations. That is the highest percentage since March 2008, when stocks were faltering under the weight of mounting mortgage defaults. The percentage was 56 percent in March 2009, when the market hit bottom.[10] Time will tell if this trend continues.

The average workplace retirement-plan participant at Vanguard Group, the biggest US mutual-fund company in terms of assets, had 72 percent allocated to stocks in 2013, up from a low of 65 percent in 2008 and four percentage points higher than 2007. But the return to stocks isn't as strong as

---

10 Joe Light, "Retirement Investors Flock Back to Stocks," *The Wall Street Journal* website, May 1, 2014, http://online.wsj.com/news/article_email/SB10001424052702303948104579535840428 373528-lMyQjAxMTA0MDAwMjEwNDIyWj.

it was near the end of the dot-com boom, when savers had around 75 percent of their portfolios in stocks.[11]

Try not to let the fear of risk and volatility keep you from experiencing the benefits of stock market growth. There are a lot of different tools on the websites of most 401(k) plans that can help you evaluate your personal risk tolerance. Just like going to a doctor, you need to talk to a professional or somebody you have trust in who has above-average knowledge to help you understand the risk. There is daily volatility in any market price, any stock market investment. Even bonds have volatility, and we cover that risk in Chapter 6. It is important to understand how volatility will impact you if you move your money out of an investment too soon.

Wait and watch. Always consult with your advisor before making a move.

Chapter 2 Summary: Key Points to Remember

1. Unlike pension plans, which are funded entirely by employers, 401(k) plans may be funded by both employers and employees. Because the employer is making the contribution on behalf of the employee, and it does a social good, the company is entitled to a tax deduction from the government for contributions it makes to employees' accounts.

2. One of the most common types of employer contributions is a match percentage. With this option, the employer will make a contribution to an employee's 401(k) account only if the employee contributes to the plan as well.

3. The employer's contributions are tax-deductible to the corporation and nontaxable to the employee. This means it is not added to the federal and state wage taxation for the employee, compliments of the US government.

4. Employee contributions are deducted from their paychecks before federal and state taxes but after Social Security taxes (excluding Pennsylvania).

5. The most important thing to remember is that one of the biggest variations among employer 401(k) plans is the formula for the employer contributions and how they match, or the percentage they might contribute to the plan.

6. Under 2016 rules, the limits are 100 percent of pay up to $18,000 for those under age fifty and $24,000 for those over the age of fifty. An employee making $15,000 per year could actually save her entire paycheck!

---

11 Ibid.

7. The Roth 401(k) is another type of retirement savings plan. The US Congress authorized it under the Internal Revenue Code, section 402A. It represents a unique combination of features of the Roth IRA and a traditional 401(k) plan. Since January 1, 2006, US employers have been allowed to amend their 401(k) plan documents to allow employees to elect a Roth IRA-type tax treatment for a portion or all of their retirement plan contributions.

8. A Roth 401(k) allows you to put money into the plan after tax. When you do that, you give up the immediate tax deduction. But the benefit is that, under the current rules, both the income from your contribution and from the growth of that money are income-tax-free later, when you retire.

9. When it makes sense to select the Roth plan depends on what you think your tax bracket might be in during retirement and also if you will need access to lump sums for large purchases. Review your current income tax bracket. If you are making less than $35,000 a year, consider contributing mostly to a Roth because you will be paying very little, if anything, in true income tax.

10. Because the Roth portion of your 401(k) account is not currently subject to income taxes at retirement, you might consider a more aggressive investment strategy on the Roth portion of your account than you do on your regular 401(k) portion. I recommend using the Roth for the most aggressive investments in your portfolio to increase the growth potential because the growth will not be taxed under current law.

11. In my work with employees, I find that their toughest decision after deciding how much to put in is to decide where to invest money.

12. Because many employees do not understand or feel qualified deciding where to invest their money, they often default to the most conservative option. By doing so, they lose out on one of the greatest miracles of the financial world, which is compound interest.

13. A lot of people think risk is related to age or life stage. I don't look at age as much as I look at the ten years before somebody retires and the five years after they retire. We call those years the "retirement hot zone" because these are the fifteen most important years in a person's investment timeline.

14. *Risk* is exposure to the chance of injury or loss, a hazard or dangerous chance, and the degree of probability of such loss. If you are worried about the "risk level" of a certain investment, you are worried about the potential permanent loss of your money. *Volatility* refers to how much your 401(k) investments can go up or down based on the performance of

the market. Volatility is less important for younger employees who have thirty to forty years until retirement because they often will not need access to the money for many years.

15. One of the most common mistakes people make with their 401(k) investments is reacting too quickly when they see movement in the market. Mixing emotions and money is often very dangerous to the performance of your account. Taking your money out of stocks to try to avoid a drop can cause you to miss out on a significant rally in the stock market.

Details That Make a Difference

All 401(k) plans are subject to federal regulation, so in some instances, the plans are similar. But the plans are also defined by each participating company's plan document, so plans often differ quite a bit based on company contributions, matching rules, the vesting schedule, what constitutes a hardship, and other details. Government regulations are not negotiable, but employers have many options regarding other details about the 401(k) programs they establish for employees.

It can be confusing because an employer you used to work for might administer its 401(k) plan a little differently than your current employer. Do not assume that all 401(k) plans are exactly alike. The first place to look for details of the plan is in the Summary Plan Description, or SPD. This document is available from your company's Human Resources Department. The SPD governs issues regarding your contributions, your employer's contributions, the vesting schedule, and whether or not 401(k) loans or hardship distributions are allowed.

In this chapter, I address those topics, as well as common questions employees have about the money they have invested in 401(k) accounts. Many of these questions revolve around how to get money out of their 401(k) accounts. Keep in mind, though, that your focus should be leaving your money in the account until retirement.

Your Contributions

Employee contributions are categorized as employee deferrals, and the tax status of those deferrals is considered to be either traditional 401(k) deferrals or Roth 401(k) deferrals. The only differences between the two are the taxability on that money when it comes out of the paycheck and when the money is paid out at retirement.

With a traditional 401(k), you contribute income pre-tax and then pay taxes on the money you withdraw. With a Roth 401(k), you pay the taxes up front so that you can make withdrawals free from federal income taxes during retirement. Here is a comparison of the tax implications of contributing to a traditional 401(k) and a Roth 401(k):

A 401(k) contribution receives a tax deduction from each paycheck. So if you put in $30 per paycheck, you will get a tax deduction on a $30 deferral. It saves you roughly 15 to 40 percent, depending on your tax bracket, on every single deposit you make—at the time the money is taken out of your paycheck. A $30 deduction might impact your take-home pay by only $20 to $25, with the difference being the tax savings. The trade-off is that, through retirement, the money builds up tax-deferred, and you must pay the tax when you pull out the money from your 401(k) account.

A Roth 401(k) contribution is different. If you put in $30, there is no immediate tax break on that contribution. A $30 contribution costs $30 from your paycheck, and then you will enjoy tax-favored withdrawals when you retire. Both the contributions and the growth on those contributions come out free from federal income taxes under current law.

The three factors that make the most impact on your decision about which 401(k) deferral is best are your age, current tax rate, and future earning potential.

For both types of plans, federal law currently caps contributions at $18,000 ($24,000 for people who are fifty or older) as of 2016.

The three factors that make the most impact on your decision about which 401(k) deferral is best are your age, current tax rate, and future earning potential.

For a young investor, a Roth account is ideal because his contributions will have a lot of time—decades—to grow free of federal income taxes. Also, a younger person is likely to increase his salary as he progresses in his career. That means the taxes he pays now are probably lower than those he will pay once he retires. Although choosing a Roth account will probably mean you will take a bigger hit on taxes now, you will receive the tax breaks at retirement. To avoid the tax hit now, many people split their contributions between a traditional 401(k) and a Roth 401(k).

Your Employer's Contributions

The Employee Retirement Income Security Act (ERISA) is a federal law that sets standards to protect individuals in private-sector retirement plans. Enacted in 1974, ERISA also sets rules regarding the federal income tax effects of transactions associated with employee benefit plans. Three government organizations share responsibility for interpreting and enforcing ERISA: the Department of Labor, the Department of the Treasury (particularly the Internal Revenue Service), and the Pension Benefit Guaranty Corporation, which deals mainly with pension plans. One of the functions of ERISA is to set the vesting schedule, which has remained the same for 401(k) plans since 2002. In the early 1990s, employers could vest benefits over a period of ten years instead of six. Then, in the late 1990s, the law changed that time period to seven years. Now employees can be fully vested within six years.

Earlier I focused on the employee contributions and the reasons why contributing is a wise idea. Now we will go through the other side of the 401(k) plan and one of the biggest benefits available: the employer contribution. An employer contribution is an investment in its employees, just the same as investing in machinery in the plant. A contribution to an employee's retirement account can be the reason employees stay or leave, and turnover is an expensive proposition for an employer. When they do make contributions, the intent is often to try to keep the best employees until retirement.

Employer contributions can be in the form of a flat dollar amount, a percentage of an employee's salary, or a "match"—a dollar amount that matches the employee's contribution. For example, a company might match 50 cents for every dollar an employee contributes, so a $20 per week contribution would receive a $10 match. If the employee puts in nothing, then there will be no employer contribution. As I mentioned earlier, these contributions are meant to keep employees for the long term, so they are not free and often come with strings attached. This is called "vesting." Many people hear the term and are often confused about what it means and why their retirement funds might be subject to it.

The Vesting Schedule

In law, "vesting" is to give an immediately secured right of present or future use. A person has a vested right to an employer contribution that the employer cannot take away, even though she may not possess the full balance yet. When the employer contribution can be transferred to the employee, it is termed a "vested interest."

Being "fully vested" means you have worked for the company long enough (six years in many organizations) that you are entitled to take 100 percent of your employer's contributions with you, along with 100 percent of your own contributions, when you leave the company.

401(k) plans give companies a competitive edge when recruiting employees through creative contribution and match formulas. It also encourages employees to stay in their jobs longer through a vesting schedule. The longer they stay employed, the more of the employer contribution they are entitled to keep if they leave or retire.

The length of vesting schedules has varied over the years, but early plan designs often started at ten years and vested 10 percent per year. Each additional year an employee stayed, he or she would get 10 percent more of the employer's contribution, eventually becoming 100 percent vested in the tenth year. A subsequent tax-law change reduced the period to seven years, with the first two years of employment being 0 percent and then 20 percent vesting for each year the employee stayed, until she was 100 percent vested in the seventh year. Today, employees typically receive 20 percent of an employer's match each year in the job and can be fully vested in six years, although some plans offer quicker vesting options.

Plans that are considered "safe harbor" allow for 100 percent immediate vesting on a portion of the employer contribution. Please check your plan provisions for complete details on your vesting schedule. These are also included in your employer's Summary Plan Description.

A sample vesting schedule is shown in the following chart. As you can see, you must work for a company for a full year before you are eligible to receive any percentage of your employer's contribution. That is pretty standard—a one-year wait and then an accumulation of 20 percent per year toward full vesting. Again, you can take 100 percent of the money you contribute, regardless of how long you stay with the company.

3-Year Cliff	
Year 1	0%
Year 2	0%
Year 3	100%

6-Year Graded	
Year 1	0%
Year 2	20%
Year 3	40%
Year 4	60%
Year 5	80%
Year 6	100%

Forfeitures—What Happens to the Unvested Money Employees Leave Behind

When an employee leaves a company before being "fully vested," or eligible to receive 100 percent of his employer's contributions, the remaining amount of the employer contribution will be reallocated to the other plan participants or used to reduce the employer contributions. Both are completely legal, and which option the company uses is determined by the plan document.

It requires education and a mind-set shift to understand that a 401(k) plan is a long-term investment account, not a short-term savings account.

Contribute It and Leave It: Early Withdrawal Is Costly

I have come across many employees who think of a 401(k) contribution as more of an easily accessible savings account than a retirement account. It requires education and a mind-set shift to understand that a 401(k) plan is a long-term investment account, not a short-term savings account. It is a retirement plan, so the contributions made to the plan are intended for retirement.

Upon termination of employment, you have the right to withdraw your own contributions and the portion of your employer's contributions you qualify for based on your years of service, but I strongly advise against it. The income taxes and penalties associated with early withdrawal are steep. Because of the tax deductions you and your employer receive, the government imposes stiff penalties if you take the money out before you retire.

If you withdraw money before you are 59½ years old, you will face three costly consequences:

1. First, you will be taxed on the amount you withdrew immediately. So the entire amount you withdraw will be added to your taxable income for the year.

2. Plus, you will pay a 10 percent penalty.

3. More importantly, you will lose the benefit of growth, or compound interest, your money could accumulate over time if you had left it in your account.

If you are in the 15 percent tax bracket and take $10,000 out of your 401(k) plan, it will be subject to income tax at 15 percent, plus a 10 percent penalty. The tax and penalty combined will be 25 percent of the amount you withdrew, or $2,500. If you are in the 20 percent tax bracket and withdraw $100,000, that might shift you into the higher 30 percent tax bracket, so you will have to pay more income tax than you would have otherwise. Plus, you will pay the 10 percent penalty, $10,000. So the total tax on your withdrawal would be $40,000. It's just not worth it!

The first two consequences are extremely costly, but the third one is the direst—the amount of growth you miss out on over time because you withdrew money early. What is extremely troubling to me is that I see many people withdrawing money from their accounts to spend on depreciating assets like a car, RV, or other consumer item.

When Can I Retire, and How Can I Avoid the 10 Percent Penalty?

You can retire at any time, assuming that your employer's plan document allows for early retirement. If it does, you could retire and take your money out to use for retirement, even at an age well before 59½. Federal rules say that if you withdraw your money and roll it into an IRA, you may avoid the immediate taxes. Under certain circumstances, you could start an income stream on that money at any time under Rule 72(t). You might also avoid the penalty if you leave the company after age fifty-five.

Rule 72(t)

We discussed the rule of 72 earlier when we discussed the rule that governs how quickly money compounds and grows. Rule 72(t) is an IRS rule that allows you to avoid paying the 10 percent penalty, but you have to roll your account to an IRA and then withdraw your money under equal and consistent period payments. The rule requires that, to take penalty-free early withdrawals, you must take at least five "substantially equal periodic payments" (SEPPs).

At age forty, that would amount to about a twenty-five- to thirty-year income stream. If you take your money out monthly for the rest of your life, you will not have to pay the 10 percent penalty. Income tax is still due on that money, but not the 10 percent penalty. This rule allows people to retire maybe at age fifty, live the lifestyle they want, and then do something with their retirement savings.

If You Quit

If you quit your job and withdraw money from your 401(k) plan, there is an alternative to paying income taxes and the penalty. You have three options:

1. You can roll the money into an individual IRA at a financial institution.

2. You can transfer your 401(k) account to your new employer's 401(k) plan, if it has one and if it allows rollovers.

3. If you have a balance of $5,000 or more in your employer's 401(k) account, you can leave the money in the plan as long as you choose.

In most situations, I advise people to transfer their 401(k) funds into their new employer's plan or, if that is not an option, to roll the balance into an IRA.

It is rarely advisable to leave your money with your previous employer's 401(k) plan.

When you leave money in a former employer's plan, that employer could make changes to the plan, or you might forget to give the former employer your new address if you move. Unless you keep in constant contact with them, there is a good chance that you can become disconnected from that 401(k) and possibly lose your money forever. The burden of proof to go back and claim the money lies on you, the employee. The IRS and Department of Labor have a process to help people match up and connect with their 401(k) plans that they have left, but it is shoddy at best. Some plans have a provision stating that an employee will forfeit his or her money to the state after a number of years. Newer regulations encourage employers to establish an IRA for these lost employees, but the burden to track down the money still lies with the employee. So regardless of the situation—even if your new employer's plan is not as modern or broad in its provisions as your previous employer's plan—it is rarely advisable to leave your money with your previous employer's 401(k) plan.

A recent Government Accounting Office (GAO) study found that only 10 to 15 percent of 401(k) plan participants who switched jobs moved their retirement savings to their new employer's 401(k) plans. That's far too few, in my opinion, because most of these people simply cashed out their balance and paid the penalties and taxes. Many employees do not weigh the cost to their retirement of doing this versus the benefit of letting the money grow. Immediate needs tend to outweigh future needs, and that is a costly approach.

Are 401(k) Plans Safe if the Employer Goes Bankrupt?

If your company goes bankrupt, your money is protected under state and federal bankruptcy laws. Once payroll contributions are deposited into the 401(k) plan, it is not subject to the creditors of the bankrupt company. The only time bankruptcy would impact a 401(k) participant is if that employer offered employees company stock as an investment option in the 401(k) plan. A lot of larger publicly traded corporations, in addition to a wide variety of mutual funds, might offer stock in that company. For example, if you work for Walmart, you could buy Walmart stock in your 401(k) plan. If that's the case, a bankruptcy of that company would impact your other account balance only because of the shares you owned. Think Enron here! But it would not impact your side-account balance if your employer goes under. Those assets are completely segregated and receive some of the most beneficial asset protections in the country.

What Should I Do when I Retire?

In most situations, when you retire, it is often advisable for you to roll your money into an IRA. Why? Because of provisions in a retirement plan that relate to beneficiary designations. For example, if I wanted to leave my proceeds to my kids over multiple generations—children, grandchildren, and great-grandchildren—I could not do that in any 401(k) plans. I can do that only through an IRA beneficiary designation because of the way current laws are written and the way most 401(k) plan documents and IRA trust agreements are written. The more money you have and the longer you want to leave the money in a qualified setting for future generations, the more favorable an IRA rollover is for you.

The more money you have and the longer you want to leave the money in a qualified setting for future generations, the more favorable an IRA rollover is for you.

Can My Spouse Contribute to My Plan?

We get this question a lot from participants. A participant will ask, for example, if his wife can roll her IRA into his 401(k) account. The answer is no. Just like an IRA—individual retirement account—is intended for one individual, a 401(k) retirement account is also owned by the individual participant. Retirement plan assets and IRA assets are generally segregated assets, meaning they belong to the participant only. There is no way to move IRAs or 401(k) plans from one spouse to another. If a participant dies, however, and his wife is the beneficiary, then she will receive the money from his account or could maintain a "spousal account" in the plan.

401(k) Loans: A Controversial Topic

Most of the people who provide retirement plans believe employees should never borrow against their retirement plan money. I am on the other team and think loans can be a great tool if used properly.

Borrowing against your 401(k) account is one of the more controversial topics when it comes to 401(k) plans. Many have put forth the reasons why employees should not borrow against their 401(k) accounts, but few are in favor of using retirement plan loans. The industry has tried to curb the amount of loans and imposed "loan origination fees" to help restrict access to loans.

So if most of the people who provide retirement plans believe employees should not borrow against their retirement plan money, why are loans still allowed? Because they allow access for employees needing money. I have seen the good and bad sides of loans, but I am firmly on the other team when it comes to loans. I think loans can be a great tool, if used properly. There are very good reasons to borrow money from a 401(k) plan, and I have advised clients to do so on many occasions. In my opinion, a 401(k) loan can make sense for many reasons, but especially in two primary scenarios:

1. For big, long-term purchases such as a business venture, a new car, or the down payment on a house

2. To pay off bad debt, such as credit cards with high interest rates

It makes perfect sense, in many cases, to take out a loan on your 401(k) plan instead of borrowing money from banks and credit card companies. If you have enough money in your 401(k) account and the provisions in the plan are favorable to the loan, you could save tens of thousands of dollars in interest that you otherwise would pay a financial institution.

When deciding whether or not to use a 401(k) loan versus a bank loan, be sure to also factor in the earnings you may lose as a result of the loan amount not being invested in your account. You will also need to consider if a loan will impact your ability to make contributions and receive the full employer matching contribution.

How Does a 401(k) Loan Work?

An employer can set up the company plan to allow employees to borrow from their accounts. Employees must have a minimum account balance before they are allowed to establish a loan. A common loan provision allows an employee the ability to borrow 50 percent of her account balance, up to a maximum of $50,000. The minimum loan under most plans is $1,000, but again, that is determined by the employer's plan documents. The loan can be paid back in weekly or monthly installments withheld from the employee's paychecks. The payback period can be as short as six months to as long as five years. However, the loan must be paid back in full if the employee terminates employment. The interest rate you will pay on the loan is determined by the plan document and is usually tied to an index of bank rates or the prime rate plus a certain percentage. This is often quite reasonable and lower than commercial rates. The best part is that the interest is paid back into your own account. You are, in effect, borrowing from yourself.

The Upside of a 401(k) Loan

Let's say you have a balance of $20,000 in your 401(k) account. You could borrow up to $10,000 from your plan. An employee with $100,000 could borrow up to the maximum of $50,000. An employee with more than $100,000 in the plan could borrow only the maximum of $50,000 as well.

The beauty of a planned participant loan is that the money is paid back to your account. The interest paid on that loan is paid to you, just like earnings. It is not paid to a bank, to the employer, or to the insurance company or mutual fund that holds the assets. Best of all, the loan is not reported to credit agencies and, if used to pay off credit cards, may even help increase credit scores, allowing you to borrow less expensively for other major purchases.

Many times, when working with employees who say they are not able to contribute to their 401(k) plan, we find that these employees often have large credit card balances. If an employee is paying a 25 percent interest rate on a credit card and has $10,000 in credit card debt, that is a huge drain on his or her finances. Many of them also pay late fees because they are behind and are not able to make their payments on time. Sometimes we find that the interest rates on these loans are as high as 25 to 30 percent. A $10,000 loan might cost the participant up to $3,000 a year to carry the credit card balance, plus late fees and other charges. A payday loan from a payroll lending company or a pawn-shop loan are often worse than the credit card companies. We have seen interest charges in excess of 50 percent with late fees and penalties.

And all too often, these same people make only the minimum payment on their credit cards, which is not enough to cover even the interest. They are making a very small dent in their debt, which makes credit card companies a lot of money. In these situations, we highly recommend that employees take a loan from their 401(k) plan to pay off the balance and then cut up the credit cards.

The following example shows how much money you could save by doing so. Let's say that you have $20,000 of credit card debt at 20 percent interest and you are making minimum payments. After ten years, your monthly payment would be $386.51, for a total of $26,381.36 of interest. If you paid it off over five years, the payments would be $529.88 per month and $11,792.66 of interest. However, if you were to have a large enough balance that you could borrow $20,000 from your 401(k) plan at a rate of 4.5 percent, your monthly payments would be $372.54. Your total interest would be only $2,371.62, and you would have paid it back into your *own* 401(k) account, not a bank!

The Downside of a 401(k) Loan

How much will a loan cost you in the long run? A $20,000 401(k) loan paid back over five years could mean you're missing out on more than $7,000 in potential earnings, according to TIAA-CREF calculations. (That's assuming that the borrower is forty years old and has twenty-five years left until retirement. It also assumes that it's a five-year loan with 6 percent loan interest and that there would have been an 8 percent return on funds over the next twenty-five years if the loan had not been taken.) [12]

That "opportunity cost" can lead to regrets. According to the National Institute of Pension Administrators (NIPA), nearly half (44 percent) of employees who took out a loan from their workplace retirement accounts later said they regretted the decision, according to TIAA-CREF's "Borrowing against Your Future" survey. An additional 23 percent of employees who took out a loan don't regret it but say they wouldn't do it again.[13]

What if an employee takes out a loan on a 401(k) account, agrees to pay it back in sixty months (five years), and then leaves the company? It is practically impossible for an employee to back out of that employee deduction, and employees rarely have the money available to pay off the loan. It is then considered an early distribution and is subject to income taxes and penalties. This is the worst-case example but unfortunately happens all too often.

Let's go back to our example of the employee who has $100,000 in his 401(k) account and takes out a $50,000 loan, the maximum amount allowed, to buy a new house. A month later, he is terminated from his job. He doesn't have the cash available to pay back the loan because he has invested all of the money in his house. That loan will be considered in default and treated as a $50,000 distribution. If his tax rate is 30 percent, he will pay that amount of tax (30 percent of $50,000 is $15,000) plus the 10 percent penalty ($5,000). That $50,000 loan has just cost the employee $20,000 in taxes and penalties. That $20,000 will be deducted from the employee's remaining $50,000. However, the $20,000 needed to pay the tax on the $50,000 loan will also be taxable. An additional $6,000 will be needed to pay this tax. This will likely leave $20,000 to $25,000 to roll over out of the original $100,000. He would still have his equity in the house, so the entire amount wouldn't be lost. However, it would still be extremely inefficient.

Unfortunately, it happens all too often.

When I counsel people about borrowing from their retirement plan, I advise them to follow three guidelines:

---

12 "401(k) Loan Regrets, National Institute of Pension Administrators blog post, July 7, 2014, http://www.nipa.org/blogpost/891501/News-from-NIPA.
13 Ibid.

1. Use 401(k) loans sparingly.

2. Use them only if you plan to be employed at that company for the entire term of the loan so that you have a paycheck from which to pay back the loan. (Of course, a layoff is beyond your control, but quitting is.)

3. Take out a loan only if you intend to follow the rules associated with it and use it to pay off what I consider to be bad debt.

I mentioned earlier that this is a controversial subject, and often I am at odds with many other advisors and plan providers about 401(k) loans. Most other providers contend that when you take out a loan on your 401(k) plan, you will lose the growth that the money could be experiencing in the market while you are paying it back. You would be taking money out of a stock market investment that could be earning a much higher rate of return. However, they often do not show the other side of the costs associated with borrowing money and the toll it might take on a family budget.

Most plans offer online loan calculators. They show that if you borrow a certain amount of money, you are anticipated to lose a certain amount of dollars in retirement income or retirement assets because you are taking that money out of the stock market. My argument is that this may or may not be the case. It really depends on a lot of other outside factors like whether the employee could actually earn that much return on the asset, whether or not there were other loans that would cause the employee to go bankrupt as a result of not being able to pay off that money, and also the higher interest and borrowing costs associated with a bad credit score.

Car Loans: Maybe

A lot of clients ask us if they should take out a 401(k) loan to buy a new car or borrow that money from a bank. Generally, if they are looking at paying more than 6 percent interest to a bank, it often makes sense to consider using a 401(k) loan for the purchase. If their bank loan will be 5 percent or less, it almost never makes sense to use a 401(k) loan.

If you plan to buy a new car and the bank is going to charge you more than 8 percent interest, it often makes sense to consider using a 401(k) loan for the purchase.

Lifestyle Loans: Rarely

It is usually not a good idea to take out a 401(k) loan to fund a lifestyle choice, such as buying a hot tub, recreational vehicle, or motorcycle. I dislike that idea because it shows that people are viewing their 401(k) plan as a savings account, not as a retirement account. Capital purchases like houses are investments that can increase in value over time, while consumer purchases often depreciate in value over time.

Hardship Distributions

A retirement plan may, but is not required to, provide for hardship distributions that allow employees to withdraw money to take care of an economic emergency. Many plans that provide for elective deferrals also provide for hardship distributions. Some 401(k) plans, 403(b) plans, and 457(b) plans permit hardship distributions.

If a 401(k) plan provides for hardship distributions, it must provide the specific criteria used to determine what constitutes a hardship. For example, an employer's plan might stipulate that a distribution can be made only for medical or funeral expenses but not for the purchase of a principal residence or for payment of tuition and education expenses.

The IRS defines a hardship as follows:

> For a distribution from a 401(k) plan to be on account of hardship, it must be made on account of an immediate and heavy financial need of the employee and the amount must be necessary to satisfy the financial need. The need of the employee includes the need of the employee's spouse or dependent.

> Whether a need is immediate and heavy depends on the facts and circumstances. Certain expenses are deemed to be immediate and heavy, including: (1) certain medical expenses; (2) costs relating to the purchase of a principal residence; (3) tuition and related educational fees and expenses; (4) payments necessary to prevent eviction from, or foreclosure on, a principal residence; (5) burial or funeral expenses; and (6) certain expenses for the repair of damage to the employee's principal residence. Expenses for the purchase of a boat or television would generally not qualify for a hardship distribution. A financial need may be immediate and heavy even if it was reasonably foreseeable or voluntarily incurred by the employee.[14]

Your primary focus should be on leaving your money in your 401(k) plan, not trying to get your money out of the plan!

Other Ways to Access Your Money

We have discussed the primary ways you can get money out of your 401(k) account: by leaving your job and taking a cash distribution instead of rolling the money over into an IRA or a new employer's 401(k) plan and by taking out a loan against your 401(k) account.

There are very few additional ways to access money from a 401(k) plan. There have been special provisions for Iraqi war veterans. In the past, veterans of war have been able to access funds for hardships that were

---

14 "Retirement Plans FAQs Regarding Hardship Distributions," IRS website, http://www.irs. gov/Retirement-Plans/Retirement-Plans-FAQs-regarding-Hardship-Distributions#2.

caused by overseas deployment. There also have been instances in which people who have been affected by major hurricanes or other major storm events have been given regional exemptions to the hardship rules to allow them to access their 401(k) account for either a direct distribution or a taxable distribution, or through loan provisions that have been expanded from $75,000 up to as much as $100,000. That is usually handled by an act of Congress, and it is usually a one-time situation in which the government makes a special provision through the IRS to allow people to access their money.

Although the focus of this chapter has been on getting your money out of your 401(k) plan, I want to stress, again, that your primary focus should be on leaving your money in your 401(k) plan! It requires a mind-set shift to recognize that it is a long-term savings plan for retirement, not a savings account. Avoiding the temptation to borrow against your account or cash it out can make the difference between a comfortable retirement and a substandard quality of life once you are no longer receiving a paycheck. Remember, the decisions you make now about your 401(k) plan will affect you for the rest of your life.

Chapter 3 Summary: Key Points to Remember

1. Do not assume that all 401(k) plans are exactly alike. The first place to look for details of your employer's plan is in the Summary Plan Description, or SPD.

2. With a traditional 401(k), you contribute income pre-tax and then pay taxes on the money when you withdraw it. With a Roth 401(k), you pay the taxes up front so that you can make withdrawals tax-free during retirement.

3. For both traditional and Roth 401(k) plans, federal law currently caps contributions at $18,000 ($24,000 for people who are fifty or older).

4. The three factors that make the most impact on your decision about which 401(k) deferral (pre-tax or Roth) is best are your age, current tax rate, and future earning potential.

5. Employer contributions can be in the form of a flat dollar amount, a percentage of an employee's salary, or a "match"—a dollar amount that matches the employee's contribution.

6. Being "fully vested" means you have worked for the company long enough (six years in many organizations) that you are entitled to take 100 percent of your employer's contributions with you, along with 100 percent of your own contributions.

7. If you withdraw money before you are 59½ years old, you will face three costly consequences. The third one is the direst. First, you will be taxed on the amount you withdrew immediately. So the entire amount you withdraw will be added to your taxable income for the year. Plus, you will pay a 10 percent penalty. More importantly, you will lose the benefit of growth, or compound interest, your money could accumulate over time if you had left it in your account. Leaving the company after age fifty-five is a way to avoid the penalty as well.

8. Rule 72(t) is an IRS rule that allows you to avoid paying the 10 percent penalty, but you have to roll your account to an IRA and then withdraw your money under equal and consistent period payments. The rule requires that, to take penalty-free early withdrawals, you must take at least five "substantially equal periodic payments" (SEPPs).

9. In most situations, when you retire, it is often advisable for you to roll your money into an IRA. If you want to leave your proceeds to your kids over multiple generations—children, grandchildren, and great-grandchildren—you can do that only with an IRA, not with any 401(k) plans.

10. Although many financial experts advise against taking out 401(k) loans, they can make sense for many reasons, but especially in two primary scenarios: (1) for big, long-term purchases such as a business venture, a new car, or the down payment on a house and (2) to pay off bad debt, such as credit cards with high interest rates.

Why Participation in a 401(k) Plan Is a Wise Decision

With pensions a luxury of the past, changes to Social Security looming on the horizon, and residential real estate values declining significantly in recent years, retirement savings accounts are just about the only way you have left to take control of the money that will sustain you when you retire.

As mentioned in the Introduction, fewer than half of US households have a retirement account, and those who do have very little saved for retirement. This is an urgent, dire situation. If you have access to an employer's 401(k) program, you are fortunate—it's easy, it reduces your taxable income, and it ensures that you will make contributions for the long term. Participating in your employer's 401(k) program is a wise move because taking advantage of this great opportunity is absolutely the best thing you can do to secure a comfortable retirement. It may also be one of the few tax deductions you have left to take advantage of—if not the only one.

Because We Can Expect Social Security Changes Soon

A lot of people think Social Security will sustain them throughout their retirement years. That is not necessarily the case. Social Security benefits are much more modest than many people realize. Based on an August 2015 article by the Center on Budget and Policy Priorities, the average Social Security retirement benefit in June 2015 was $1,335 a month, or a bit over $16,000 in a year. For someone who worked all of his or her adult life at an average earnings of $50,000 per year and retires at age sixty-five in 2015, Social Security benefits replace about 40 percent of past earnings. This "replacement rate" will slip to about 36 percent for a medium earner retiring at sixty-five in the future, chiefly because the full retirement age, which has already risen to sixty-six, will climb to sixty-seven over the 2017–22 period.[15]

We believe the current Social Security program will change substantially, whether that will include "means testing," a reduction of benefits, or elimination of cost-of-living increases.

In our role as financial advisors, we encourage people to take a realistic view about Social Security. Those who are within ten years of applying for Social Security could see their benefits cut by 10 percent, based on projections from

15 http://www.cbpp.org/sites/default/files/atoms/files/PolicyBasics_SocSec-TopTen.pdf

45

the Social Security Administration. We believe the current Social Security program will change substantially, whether that will include "means testing," a reduction of benefits, or elimination of cost-of-living increases. *Means testing* simply refers to adjusting benefits based on the recipient's "means" or financial condition. In effect, the more you have, the less you would receive in benefits.

It is our opinion that we cannot use the Social Security base as retirement income to the same extent as we did in the past. The government may be forced to mandate changes of some sort. If someone is expecting to receive $20,000 a year in income from Social Security, we are recommending that they cut that by $5,000 and use $15,000 as the Social Security base for their income projections. And, for those retirees who will receive the maximum Social Security income payment, which is about $2,500 a month, we are advising them that their payments are likely to be reduced, either through taxation or benefit reduction. For those employees who are ten or fifteen years from retirement, we are recommending that they plan for a 25 percent cut in Social Security benefits.

Retirement savings accounts are becoming an increasingly important part of Americans' income stream after they stop working. Contributing as much as you can to your 401(k) account while you are still working is a critical investment in your future.

Because Home Real Estate Value Is No Longer a Reliable Retirement Asset

Many people who retired during the last century relied on their homes as a source of retirement income. After living in their home, they would sell it and downsize as they entered retirement, using those extra reserves to support an income stream in retirement. Unfortunately, because of recent drastic fluctuations in the real estate market, we can no longer rely on this as a stable source of retirement income. Because your home may not be worth as much as you planned heading into retirement, the ideal situation would be to have your home paid for by the time you retire. However, about 30 percent of homeowners ages sixty-five and older carried a mortgage in 2011, the most recent data available. That figure increased from 22 percent in 2001.[16] This adds to the cost of retirement, which adds to the amount of money many will need to support their income needs.

Also, a home has a low risk/reward ratio. Real estate can be slow to recover after a downturn. For example, the S&P lost 58 percent of its value before bottoming out in March 2009. It has since recovered to a level that is 13 percent above its pre-crisis peak. In comparison, the US real estate market fell about 35 percent from its peak and is now well below its pre-crisis peak. In some states, such as Florida, homes lost more than 50 percent from the

---

16 Susan Tompor, "Rethink Your Finances and Retirement Risks," USA Today website, May 25, 2014, http://www.usatoday.com/story/money/columnist/tompor/2014/05/25/susan-tompor-rethink-your-finances-and-retirement-risks/9514391/.

peak and have not fully recovered.[17] This has caused many people to delay retirement and continue working past their original planned retirement date.

Another source of retirement value available on your home might be a "reverse mortgage." Due to the complexities of these arrangements, I will not fully discuss their options here other than to say that most employees planning for retirement would often be better off planning to save the needed amount into their 401(k) plan so that the sale of the home for retirement income will not be needed.

There are just no guarantees of enough future value with residential real estate.

Because of Longevity Risk

When planning how much money you'll need in retirement, it's important to consider "longevity risk." You may need to save more money than you think. According to the Social Security Administration, a man who reaches age 65 today can expect to live, on average, until age 84.3, and a woman who reaches age 65 can expect to live until age 86.6. One out of every four sixty-five-year-olds today will live past age ninety, and one out of ten will live past age ninety-five.[18]

Those are just averages, of course. Tom Hegna, a speaker, economist, and former senior executive officer of a Fortune 100 company, says averages are not at all an indicator of how long your retirement days will last. Here is what he advises in his book *Paychecks and Play Checks*: "

> When planning for retirement income, you cannot plan to have income until age ninety—you really need to plan to have income until age one hundred and possibly beyond. That may seem like playing it a bit too safe, but it is not at all unreasonable if half of retirees are already living into their nineties. Your retirement savings will probably need to last for twenty-five years or more. In addition, the longer you live, the more inflation can eat away at your savings if you are not careful. You will need an investment and withdrawal strategy that will last as long as you do.[19]

When people from pension funds or life insurance companies talk about "longevity risk," they are referring to the increasing life expectancy of policyholders and those who receive pensions, which can result in payout

17 Matthew Frankel, "Here's Why Your Home Isn't a Good Investment and Won't Help You Retire Rich," The Motley Fool website, January 4, 2014, http://www.fool.com/investing/general/2014/01/04/heres-why-your-home-isnt-a-good-investment-and-won.aspx.

18 "Calculators: Life Expectancy," Social Security Administration website, http://www.ssa.gov/planners/lifeexpectancy.htm.

19 Tom Hegna, *Paychecks and Play Checks: Retirement Solutions for Life* (Boston: Acanthus Publishing, 2011). This excerpt is from Chapter 2 on Tom Hegna's website, http://www.paychecksandplaychecks.com/sample-chapter.html.

levels that are higher than they planned for. It can affect the solvency of a plan significantly. But when we talk about longevity risk in the context of individual plan participants, it refers to the risk that a person will outlive her retirement savings.

People are living longer than they used to, which means we all need to fund more years past retirement than our parents did. And with longevity comes the added risk that we might become sick or disabled and need medical care and long-term care. That will increase the amount of money needed in retirement considerably.

To try to predict how long you might live, look at your current lifestyle and the longevity of your parents, which gives you at least a road map of what your genetic makeup is like. A person who is sixty years old is not likely to live to be ninety-five unless he had grandparents, parents, aunts, and uncles who have made it to that age. As a general rule, we advise people to plan to have enough money to sustain them for at least thirty years after they retire.

Consider an Annuity

Longevity risk is the main reason people under-retire. When people go into retirement, many of them are afraid to keep their money invested fully in the stock market, so they substantially reduce their market risk by investing elsewhere. An annuity can help you absorb some of that risk, and it is something wise to consider because it may provide you with a steady income stream in retirement. However, the expenses can be high in certain variable annuities, and the payouts on income annuities vary greatly from company to company, so investigate your options thoroughly with an advisor before you consider purchasing one.

> **Disclaimer: Variable annuities are long-term investments suitable for retirement funding and are subject to market fluctuations and investment risk, including the possibility of loss of principal. Variable annuities are sold by prospectus, which contains information about the variable annuity, including a description of applicable fees and charges. These include, but are not limited to, mortality and expense risk charges, administrative fees, and charges for optional benefits and riders. The prospectus can be obtained from the insurance company offering the variable annuity or from your financial professional. Read it carefully before you invest. Guarantees are based on the financial strength and claims paying ability of the insurance company.**

Income Annuities as a 401(k) Plan Option

Individual annuities have traditionally not been available as an option within a 401(k) plan; you would need to buy one separately, as a supplemental retirement investment.

Money invested in an annuity will make payments on a future date or series of dates—monthly, quarterly, annually, or in a lump-sum payment. You can opt to receive payments for the rest of your life or for a set number of years. The size of the payments is determined by factors such as the length of the payment period, your account balance, and expected yield. It also depends on whether you choose a guaranteed payout (a "fixed income annuity") or a payout stream determined by the performance of your annuity's investments (a "variable income annuity").

If you purchase an annuity with a guaranteed income stream, you take your money out of the investment risk side and you get what is called a "mortality bonus." For example, most financial planning experts consider a 4.5 to 5 percent distribution rate to be the preferred rate. So if you have $1 million, that means a maximum annual withdrawal of $45,000 to $50,000. An annuity will have a payout ratio of 8.5 to 9 percent for that same individual. That is guaranteed to pay out for the life of the annuitant and will never end. An annuity is a way to guarantee that you will not outlive a portion of your income. And it allows you to invest the rest of your money a little more aggressively, knowing you have something to fall back on. It's not a blanket recommendation, and it depends on individual circumstances, but it is something we advise a lot of people to consider.

Longevity Insurance: A Relatively New Option

In the past few years, a type of annuity available inside a 401(k) plan has increased in popularity as a way to help people ensure they don't outlive their money. This type of annuity is called a Deferred Income Annuity (DIA)[20], and it is sometimes referred to as "longevity insurance." Now federal regulations give the government's "blessing" to the concept of longevity insurance.

New rules that the US Treasury Department issued on July 1, 2014, give retirees with 401(k) plans and IRAs more flexibility to purchase annuities that don't start paying out until age eighty or eighty-five. The

New rules that the US Treasury Department issued on July 1, 2014, give retirees with 401(k) plans and IRAs more flexibility to purchase annuities that don't start paying out until age eighty or eighty-five.

---

20 It is important to understand that annuities are not appropriate for qualified money if the only benefit of the purchase is tax deferral. Annuities are also not intended for short-term investors or situations in which required minimum distributions would result in a withdrawal charge. However, annuities may be appropriate for qualified plans when tax deferral isn't the only thing an investor is considering.

new rules provide a new way for retirees to limit the drawdowns of their account balances that are required starting after age 70½. Now they can use as much as 25 percent of their account balances up to $125,000 to purchase deferred annuities. The Treasury Department says about one in five 401(k) plans offers annuities as a choice.[21]

In 2012, for the first time, sales of this type of annuity offering longevity insurance topped $1 billion, according to LIMRA, a market research firm. Sales were 160 percent higher in the fourth quarter of 2012 than they were in the first quarter of the year.[22]

In general, DIAs require policyholders to pick an income start date in the future. Start dates can range from one to forty or more years from purchase. When you buy longevity insurance through a DIA, you pay a lump sum of money today, and the insurance company guarantees you an amount of monthly income at a specified future age, often age eighty-five or ninety. A deferred income annuity purchased with $100,000 at the age of seventy would be expected to provide annual payments, starting at the age of eighty-five, of $26,000 to $42,000. The amount will depend on the interest rate, whether a joint-and-survivor annuity was chosen, and other factors. If the purchase was made at the age of sixty-five, the $42,000 figure would increase to $51,000.[23]

Income-based annuities offer a lot of security, but there are risks, most notably the "use it or lose it" stipulation. Most policies do not include a death benefit, so if you die before the date on which your benefits were scheduled to begin, your heirs receive nothing; the insurance company keeps the money.

Two Methods for Predicting the Income You'll Need
In the financial-planning world, there are two methods of projecting a person's needed income stream at retirement: "principal preservation" and "principal depletion." An income annuity is one form of principal depletion.

1. Principal Preservation
With the principal preservation income approach, the goal is to provide an income stream that does not encroach on or use any of your principal during retirement. So if you retire with $1 million, the goal is to ensure that there will always be at least $1 million there, and you can take an income stream from that amount or more. This allows for not only the distribution of your income over a thirty-year period; it also provides for possible growth to accommodate future inflation.

21 "Treasury: Retirement Accounts Can Include Longevity Annuities to Limit Drawdowns," Bloomberg News website, July 1, 2014, http://www.fa-mag.com/news/annuities-in-u-s--retirement-plans-get-boost-from-u-s--treasury-18466.html.
22 Brent Hunsberger, "Longevity insurance: Keep Your Eyes Open when Buying," The Oregonian website, April 27, 2013, *http://www.oregonlive.com/finance/index.ssf/2013/04/longevity_insurance_keep_your.html.
23 John A. Turner, PhD, and David D. McCarthy, "Longevity Insurance Annuities in 401(k) Plans and IRAs," Benefits Quarterly report, First Quarter 2013, International Foundation of Employee Benefit Plans (IFEBP) website, http://www.ifebp.org/inforequest/0163295.pdf.

In effect, it allows for an inflated income distribution. In the early years, you may be earning a 6 or 7 percent return on your account but might be taking out only 4 or 5 percent. So it allows 2 or 3 percent to reinvest for about the first fifteen years. In the last fifteen years of your retirement, all of the extra money that is reinvested continues to grow and allows for an increasing income stream but ends up at $1 million again.

2. Principal Depletion

The second type of income planning, principal depletion, allows for a little higher distribution, but it uses or depletes principal for that higher amount. This might be an option for people who need maximum income in retirement or for people who are not concerned about leaving an inheritance for heirs when they die.

The mathematical projection is almost like a mortgage in reverse—not a reverse mortgage, but a mortgage in reverse. When you borrow $500,000 to buy a house, the bank calculates what the interest will be over a thirty-year period and then backs into how much of a monthly payment you will need to make to get that to zero in the thirtieth year. In planning retirement distribution using a depletion method, we project that, say, in thirty years, a participant is going to have a zero account balance. We would project an interest rate for the growth and then a time period over which the income would be used. The model then gives us the amount available to withdraw as income each year over that period, leaving nothing at the end. This is a riskier approach because it allows very little room for error. If you experience bad years in the market or years in which you incur unexpected expenses such as medical bills and need to pull extra money from your account, you could run out of money too soon. I rarely recommend the depletion approach unless a person does not have enough money saved to support his or her lifestyle during retirement.

Because the Tax Benefits Are Significant

The tax benefits available from both a traditional 401(k) and a Roth 401(k) are tremendous. Investing in a 401(k) plan is one of the few ways the average wage-earning citizen of the United States can find tax deductions for savings.

Investing in a 401(k) plan is one of the few ways the average wage-earning US citizen can find tax deductions for savings.

With the saver's tax credit available to participants in the lower income categories, 401(k) participants could even earn income tax credits for contributing to their retirement. A credit is different from a deduction in that it is an actual contribution from the government meant to incentivize employees to participate in their plan.

The saver's tax credit (formally known as the Retirement Savings Contributions Credit) is a tax credit available to low to moderate-income

51

taxpayers who save for retirement in 401(k) plans and individual retirement accounts. It is worth as much as $1,000 for individuals and $2,000 for couples. You can claim the saver's credit in addition to the tax deduction you get for contributing to a traditional 401(k) or IRA.

The credit is available to single taxpayers, married taxpayers who are filing separately, and qualifying widows or widowers with incomes up to $27,750; heads of household with incomes up to $41,625; and married couples filing jointly with incomes up to $55,500.

Your credit amount is based on your filing status, adjusted gross income, tax liability, and amount contributed to qualifying retirement programs. IRS Form 8880 is used to claim the saver's credit. For more information from the IRS about this credit, visit http://www.irs.gov/uac/Get-Credit-for-Your-Retirement-Savings-Contributions.

Tax benefits are also available with an IRA, but the amount of the contribution is limited, compared to a 401(k). For 2016, the maximum you can contribute to all of your traditional and Roth IRAs is $5,500 ($6,500 if you're age fifty or older) or your taxable compensation for the year, whichever is less. The IRA contribution limit does not apply to rollover contributions or qualified reservist repayments.[24]

When making a contribution to a traditional IRA or 401(k), most people get an up-front tax deduction, reducing their taxable income and, as a result, leading to either a bigger refund or a smaller tax bill. Then the investments within their retirement accounts grow on a tax-deferred basis, meaning that any income they generate—interest, dividends, or capital gains—doesn't get taxed immediately. Those benefits alone can cut thousands of dollars off the total amount of taxes you pay between now and retirement.

But the trade-off for all of those tax benefits that retirement accounts offer is that when you withdraw money from a traditional IRA or 401(k) account, you have to pay tax on the withdrawal. With only a couple of rare exceptions, you always pay your ordinary income tax rate on money you withdraw from a retirement account. That can be much higher than the rate you would pay on dividends and long-term capital gains. It exposes a hidden tax cost for putting certain assets into retirement accounts rather than using taxable accounts.[25]

As mentioned earlier, with a traditional IRA, you pay taxes when you withdraw the money in retirement. However, with a Roth IRA, taxes are paid up front on the contributions. Also, you may not be eligible for a Roth IRA if your income is more than $132,000 (single filer) or $194,000 (joint filer) in 2016.

Because You Can Combine 401(k) Plans

During our education meetings, we come across many people who have 401(k) accounts and IRAs from previous jobs that are often in expensive investments

---

24 "Retirement Topics—IRA Contribution Limits," IRS website, http://www.irs.gov/Retirement-Plans/Plan-Participant,-Employee/Retirement-Topics-IRA-Contribution-Limits.
25 Dan Caplinger, "The Hidden Tax Cost of Retirement Accounts," The Motley Fool, July 10, 2014.

or subject to heavy fees. One of the biggest advantages to today's 401(k) plans is that they almost always allow rollovers from other plans and IRAs. Under the new rules, you may be able to roll over just about any previous retirement plan, other than a government 457 plan. You can roll over IRAs, old 401(k) plans, old defined-benefit plans, and even simple IRA plans into a 401(k) plan that allows for rollovers, allowing you to consolidate these various accounts into one manageable account. This new flexibility allows employees to merge all of their assets into one account to help simplify and control the process of retirement saving.

You cannot, however, roll over a personal Roth account into a company-sponsored 401(k) Roth. That's because of some timing deadlines that stipulate when you can take money out of an individual Roth. For both individual Roth accounts and 401(k) accounts, you must complete a five-year "non-exclusion" period to be eligible to receive a tax-free distribution. This period is five tax years after you make your first Roth 401(k) deposit. The non-exclusion period begins on the first day of the first taxable year in which you make contributions into your Roth plan.

Let's say you make your first Roth 401(k) contribution on August 1, 2014. The non-exclusion period starts on January 1, 2014, the first day of the 2014 taxable year. The five-year rule basically states that five tax years must pass from when your first contribution is made to any Roth IRA before a qualified distribution can be made. This varies from an individual Roth IRA in that the time starts on the date of the first deposit.

So, if you rolled your personal Roth into a 401(k) Roth, there would be no way to track that five-year time frame. That is why the government does not allow personal Roth accounts to be rolled into 401(k) Roths.

Rolling other types of accounts into your employer's 401(k) plan offers, in general, lower investment fees and expenses than an individual IRA does. Individual mutual funds often carry up-front sales loads and additional fees that are higher than they are in a 401(k) plan. I recommend that you compare the fee ratios of your current investments to your 401(k) plan. You might be able to cut your investment fees significantly by rolling them into your 401(k) plan. If you are in traditional investments like CDs, or other low-yielding types of IRAs, often you may be able to get another 1, 2, or even 3 percent more yield inside of a 401(k) plan's fixed-investment feature.

Rolling other types of accounts into your employer's 401(k) plan offers, in general, lower investment fees and expenses than an individual IRA does.

We have had many situations in which participants have a large amount of money in an IRA at a bank or other institution that is paying a very low interest rate. They were able to move that money into their 401(k) plan and increase their fixed-interest return by a couple of percentage points or more. The investment risk is similar, but getting 2 or 3 percent more on their money substantially increases their return. The most important thing to consider is that a 401(k) does not usually offer any account that provides FDIC coverage on deposits, and the fixed accounts are often backed by the strength of an insurance company. It's simply a matter of comparing interest rates and evaluating the risk associated with the lack of FDIC coverage to determine if this option is right for you.

Another benefit is that this type of rollover is flexible. An IRA rolled into the plan often can be rolled back out of the plan, as well back into an IRA, or even for direct distribution. Let's say that, two years after you roll an IRA into the plan, your bank is running an interest-rate special. You would be able to move the money back into an IRA, and you could receive the higher interest rate without paying a penalty. That is the only time employees can take a rollout while still being employed, unless they are over the age of 59½.

Because You Don't Have to Make $1 Million to Become a 401(k) Millionaire

This country now has more "retirement plan millionaires" than at any time in history. In fact, a twenty-five-year-old employee who makes just $30,000 per year could accumulate more than $1 million by age sixty-five by contributing just 10 percent of his income! This assumes that his investment earns an 8 percent rate of return with a 2 percent salary increase through retirement.

Fidelity recently studied more than one thousand people who had more than $1 million in their Fidelity-managed 401(k) accounts to see what strategies worked for them. All of them earned less than $150,000 a year. The researchers looked at twelve years of these investors' saving history, from 2000 to 2012. They found five habits common among 401(k) millionaires. They:

1. Start saving early

2. Contribute a minimum of 10 to 15 percent of their salaries

3. Meet their employer match amounts

4. Consider mutual funds that invest in stocks

5. Do not cash out when changing jobs

The study found that the average age of these 401(k) millionaires is fifty-nine, and they have worked at their respective companies for more than thirty years.[26]

A 401(k) plan is a wise idea because it is the simplest way to accumulate money—the contributions are taken out of your paycheck automatically. The process is taken out of the hands of a human and put into automation, which is much more reliable because no emotion is involved in the process. The key

26 "Five Habits of 401(k) Millionaires," Fidelity website, January 2, 2014, https://www.fidelity.com/viewpoints/retirement/how-to-become-a-millionaire-with-a-401k.

to any retirement savings program is not so much the yield on the money as much as it is your ability to continue to put the money away. Most savings programs are very difficult to stick with for thirty or forty years simply because they are subject to the whims and purchases of a participant. It requires that you be disciplined enough, on a consistent basis, to write a check every month for a savings contribution. People have good intentions—they mean to put away $10,000 a year on their own, but things come up, and instead, they use the money to buy cars, go on trips, or help their children out.

We can't say it enough: start early, contribute as much as possible, and leave the money in your 401(k) plan for as long as possible.

Chapter 4 Summary: Key Points to Remember

1. One reason that saving for retirement is more important than ever is because we most likely cannot use the Social Security base as retirement income to the same extent as we did in the past. The average woman who was sixty-five or older received only $12,520 in Social Security benefits in 2012.

2. Another reason Americans need to save for retirement is because we no longer can rely on our homes as a source of retirement income. Recent drastic fluctuations in the real estate market have made real estate an unstable source of retirement income.

3. A third reason we need to save for retirement is because of "longevity risk." In the context of individual plan participants, this term refers to the risk that a person will outlive her retirement savings. People are living longer than they used to, which means we all need to fund more years of retirement than our parents did. And with longevity comes the added risk that we might become sick or disabled and need medical care and long-term care. That will increase the amount of money needed in retirement considerably.

4. To try to predict how long you might live, look at your current lifestyle and the longevity of your parents, which gives you at least a road map of what your genetic makeup is like.

5. An annuity can help you absorb some of the risk associated with stock market fluctuation. It may provide you with a steady income stream in retirement. However, the expenses can be high in certain variable annuities, and the payouts on income annuities vary greatly from company to company, so investigate your options thoroughly with an advisor before you consider purchasing one.

6. In the past few years, a type of annuity available inside a 401(k) plan has increased in popularity as a way to help people ensure they don't outlive their money. This type of annuities is called a Deferred Income Annuity (DIA), and it is sometimes referred to as "longevity insurance." Now federal regulations give the government's "blessing" to the concept of longevity insurance.

7. Investing in a 401(k) plan is one of the few ways the average wage-earning citizen of the United States can find tax deductions for savings.

8. The saver's tax credit (formally known as the Retirement Savings Contributions Credit) is a tax credit available to low to moderate-income taxpayers who save for retirement in 401(k) plans and individual retirement accounts. It is worth as much as $1,000 for individuals and $2,000 for couples. You can claim the saver's credit in addition to the tax deduction you get for contributing to a traditional 401(k) or IRA.

9. One of the biggest advantages to today's 401(k) plans is that they almost always allow rollovers from other plans and IRAs. This flexibility allows employees to merge all of their assets into one account to help simplify and control the process of retirement saving.

10. This country now has more "retirement plan millionaires" than at any time in history. In fact, a twenty-five-year-old employee who makes just $30,000 per year could accumulate more than $1 million by age sixty-five by contributing just 10 percent of his income!

CHAPTER 5

How Should I Invest My Money?

Please note: The information contained in this chapter should not be construed as financial advice. Each investor's situation is different. Please consult with your financial advisor regarding specific investment strategies that are applicable to your personal financial situation.

Earlier, I mentioned that the biggest problem people have with 401(k) plans is knowing how much money to contribute. The second biggest problem participants have is knowing how to invest in a plan. Most people consider asset allocation a mystery. They do not know how much of their contribution to invest in stock funds, bond funds, or cash, mostly because they don't understand how stock and bond markets work.

People tend to perceive the 401(k) as either a massive benefit or a massive disservice, based on their own perceptions of these markets. My objective in writing this book is to help clarify some of the misconceptions people have about investments and the role they play in your 401(k) plan.

To qualify as offering full diversification, a 401(k) plan can have only three types of investment options:

1. A growth option, which is generally a stock-market investment (stocks)

2. A bond-market investment option, which is a fixed-income option (bonds)

3. Some type of stable-value or fixed-interest option (cash)

Most plans today offer anywhere from five to five hundred different investment options. It has been our experience that the more investment options are available, the more confused participants become and the less they participate in the plan. The choices become overwhelming when participants are forced to research the various funds and make a choice that will determine their retirement lifestyle.

Let's explore some of the common misconceptions about investing in general and discuss some strategies that will help you navigate this part of the 401(k) process. I have included in the Appendix a list of definitions of various types of investments, including bonds and stock funds.

Balancing Risk with Reward

As you look at the investment options in your 401(k) plan, the most important question to ask yourself is "How much risk am I willing to take between now and the time I will need to start an income stream for retirement?" The more time you have before retirement, the more you can afford the daily volatility of the stock market and the risk associated with it, thereby exposing your account to possible higher yields. And generally, the more stock-market risk you can afford to take, the higher potential rates of return you can get. Generally, participants favor stock-market investments because historical averages over long time frames have favored stock-market or equity types of investments.

As a participant, the goal should be to balance risk with reward, or return on investment. When first enrolling in a 401(k) plan—maybe when you are hired at your first job out of college—you select your investment mix based on the level of risk you are comfortable with, your age, how close you are to retirement, and what type of lifestyle you want to have when you retire. You want to reach retirement with as much money as possible while incurring the least amount of risk possible. So you choose a mix of stocks, bonds, and cash based on your retirement goals. As time passes, those assets grow at different rates because they all react to the same market conditions differently and become out of alignment with the allocation you initially chose. For that reason, it is important to rebalance your assets once a year—quarterly at most.

Reallocation vs. Rebalancing

People often use the terms "reallocation" and "rebalancing" interchangeably, but they are entirely different concepts. *Reallocation* is when you change the percentage of assets, or the "allocation," you have invested in those three asset classes (stocks, bonds, cash). We rarely advocate reallocating often—only when your risk level or need for income changes. *Rebalancing* is when you sell or buy funds in your plan so that your asset-allocation percentages remain consistent and in line with your original choices. We recommend that you rebalance your account at least once a year—quarterly at most. Rebalancing too often might cause you to incur a plan-level fee or even trigger a market timing period in which you might not be able to change your investments for a set period of time. This is common for people who are trying to "time" the market. The regulators have strict rules that govern and attempt to limit this practice. For longer-term investment strategies, a 401(k) will allow you to come in and out of investments as often as you should, but never more than you should.

Most participants ignore rebalancing entirely. According to David Wray, president of the Plan Sponsor Council of America, 80 percent of people don't rebalance their 401(k) accounts.[27] It is common for a plan participant to enroll in a plan at a young age, select an allocation, and never rebalance the investment mix!

Here is an example of how rebalancing resets your assets to your original allocation. Let's say you have decided on a portfolio of 60 percent equities, 35 percent bonds, and 5 percent cash. If equity prices increase, the equity portion of your portfolio might rise to 65 percent, and fixed income will decrease to 30 percent. Or the market might decline, and your allocation might end up being 55 percent equities and 40 percent bonds. Rebalancing back to your initial allocation levels resets your account to your original risk exposure and expected return. In both examples, rebalancing will correct your asset allocation back to 60 percent equities and 35 percent fixed income.

When using a rebalance strategy, you are selling equities after gains and buying equities after losses. But many investors do just the opposite—they buy after gains and sell after losses. It might seem logical to sell an investment that has performed poorly only to buy more of an investment that has performed well. But that may be a costly mistake, and it is wise to do exactly the opposite. Rebalancing helps investors buy low and sell high on a systematic basis, if only in small increments.

During the 2008–09 market correction, many investors were riding high on a five-year market recovery after the Internet bubble burst earlier in the decade. Many investors thought stocks would keep rising, but they did not. This unfounded optimism left investors unprepared for the risks of the subsequent downturn.

Automatic Rebalancing Makes It Simple

A simple and useful but much-underused tool is the automatic rebalancing feature available in many 401(k) plans. This online tool removes the guesswork from how and when to rebalance your account. According to Aon Hewitt, just 9 percent of 401(k) participants who have access to this auto-rebalancing feature take advantage of it.[28] If the stock market posts big gains and your stock-market allocation rises from the 50 percent you originally allocated to 70 percent, this possibly exposes you to additional risk. If you enable

A simple and useful tool is the automatic rebalancing feature available in many 401(k) plans. It removes the guesswork from how and when to balance your account, yet only 9 percent of the participants who have access to this feature take advantage of it.

---

27 "Boost Your 401(k) Returns by Rebalancing," 401khelpcenter.org, http://www.401khelpcenter.com/401k_education/401k_rebalancing.html#.U5jQuyggtxg.

28 Barry Glassman, CFP®, "The Biggest and Costliest 401(k) Mistakes People Make and How to Avoid Them," Glassman Wealth Services website, May 28, 2014, http://www.glassmanwealth.com/biggest-costliest-401k-mistakes.

the automatic rebalancing feature, then at predesignated times—for example, once or twice a year—your account will automatically reset your allocation to the percentages you originally started out with.

Before this feature was available, plan participants had to rebalance manually. In the early 1990s, most 401(k) plans had limited stock-market options. In our practice, we recognized early on that employees were not only uncomfortable making the decision about where to invest their money; they were also often unqualified to make investment choices. So, before plans were offering automatic rebalancing of asset allocation, we designed our own models and literally drew them on people's enrollment applications. We would offer four different risk-adjusted models: aggressive, moderate, conservative, and stable value. We would discuss with each participant how aggressive an investor he or she is. Then they would simply check one of four boxes that would automatically default them into a portfolio. We were one of few companies that offered that type of option at that time. Knowing how much difficulty participants were having selecting an investment portfolio, we have always tried to make asset allocation as simple as possible for them.

Over the years, plan managers began to recognize that investors were uncomfortable about making investment decisions and were often unqualified to do so. So they began to offer predetermined models or asset-allocation funds and selection based on investors' risk levels. Now, with today's new target-date funds, plans are offering investments that are dynamic and change allocations as participants get older.

A Cycling Analogy: Three Types of Investors

When discussing the investment options during our participant meetings, I will often use an analogy of a unicycle, a bicycle, and a tricycle to describe the three basic types of investors and their investment philosophies. Because investing is a very difficult process for many people to visualize, I help them see the similarities between developing a portfolio and trying to ride three different types of cycles.

1. **Unicycle investors**—A unicycle is very difficult to learn, but once you master it and finally get on it, it's all about balance. It is similar to developing an individual portfolio within a plan's many options. Once a participant gains his balance with this type of portfolio, he can simply adjust his balance over time. He can adjust his lower or higher as he sees fit. Highly savvy investors usually prefer to make their own investment decisions. They also make up the smallest percentage of participants. To accommodate them, we like to offer from fifteen to twenty-five individual investment options that cover most of the investment styles and risk levels, from aggressive international funds to conservative choices. We want the knowledgeable participants to have ample choices so they can cover most any allocation.

2. **Bicycle investors**—It is easier to learn how to ride a bicycle than a unicycle. Once you are able to mount and pedal a bicycle, all you need to decide is where and when you want to turn or stop. This mid-level of difficulty is like determining the risk level of where an investor is today: ultra-aggressive, aggressive, moderate-aggressive, moderate, or conservative. The portfolios are predetermined for them and are made up of a mixture of twenty to forty different individual investment choises that match the investor's level of risk. After choosing which allocation is best for them, they simply need to determine when they need to make a "turn" or adjust the portfolio or when to stop it altogether and move to a different allocation.

3. **Tricycle investors**—A tricycle is the easiest of the three types of cycles to ride. The only choice is to determine how fast you want to go; you do not need to worry about "balance." The tricycle is designed to remove most of the risk of balancing the ride. Similar to a tricycle, a "target date" type of investment removes the need for a participant to rebalance his portfolio and sets him up to do it automatically. A participant choosing this type of investment is often the least investment-savvy or is simply a participant who feels comfortable with investing but chooses not to do it. A target-date style investment is a predetermined portfolio that automatically rebalances as the participant gets closer to a predetermined date, usually retirement.

> *A "target date" type of investment removes the need for a participant to rebalance his portfolio and sets him up to do it automatically.*

Here is an example of how it might work. The participant would set a retirement date for the year closest to 2020, 2030, 2040, or 2050—any date in the future. Some plans offer five-year increments as well. The investment manager will design a portfolio allocation, and then each year, the manager automatically reduces the risk in the portfolio to make it a little more conservative, with less money invested in stocks. At about ten years before that retirement date, the risk of that portfolio starts to decrease substantially.

Let's say a thirty-year-old decides to retire in 2050. The target-date portfolio would allocate about 95 percent of the portfolio into stock-market types of investments and about 5 percent in more conservative investments. Ten years from now, it would adjust to 85 percent stocks and 15 percent bonds and conservative allocation. Then in twenty years, it might adjust to 70 percent stocks and 30 percent bonds. When that investor finally reaches retirement in 2050, the portfolio may have about 60 percent of the investments in stocks and 40 percent in more conservative investments. Contrary to what most participants believe, it is rarely advisable to come completely out of stocks as they are retiring because most people will need to have some money at risk, or in the stock market, to offset the risk of inflation eroding their savings and income potential.

According to research by the Employee Benefit Research Institute (EBRI) and the Investment Company Institute (ICI), the number of 401(k) plan participants who are investing in target-date style investments is increasing. Based on a study by the Investment Company Institute in 2014, 60 percent of 401(k) participants in their twenties held target-date funds, compared with 41 percent of 401(k) participants in their sixties. The study also found that recently hired participants (two or fewer years of tenure) used target-date funds—59 percent of recently hired 401(k) participants held target-date funds, compared with 48 percent of 401(k) plan participants overall.[29] In 2012, 41 percent of 401(k) participants held target-date investments, up from 39 percent in 2011 and 19 percent in 2006. In addition, 15 percent of the assets in the EBRI/ ICI 401(k) database were invested in these styles of investment choices at year-end 2012, up from 13 percent in 2011 and 5 percent in 2006.[30]

Long-Term vs. Short-Term Investing

One of the most important pieces of advice I have for 401(k) plan participants is this: "When you get *into* the market is not nearly as important as when you *come out* of the market."

Many of the participants we have worked with over the years confuse normal market fluctuations with market cycles. I try to explain that this is similar to the difference between the weather on any given day versus the climate of the state in which you live. If you live in Miami or Seattle, it is often wise to carry an umbrella to protect yourself from an occasional rain shower. This is "weather protection" because the umbrella is there to protect you from the rain if it comes, but most of the time it will rain. However, if you live in Minneapolis in the winter, you will most certainly need to wear a heavy, insulated coat in January. This is "climate protection" because of the climate of the Minnesota region. While there may be a warm day from time to time, January in Minnesota is most likely going to be very cold, and you must wear a coat at all times when outside.

Designing a portfolio for short-term ups and downs (similar to weather changes) is not as effective or efficient as protecting yourself from the big changes in the economy (similar to the climate). The short-term ups and downs

29 "401(k) Plan Asset Allocation, Account Balances, and Loan Activity in 2014," www.ici. org/401k/news/16_news_ebri_ici_target.

30 Jack VanDerhei, Sarah Holden, Luis Alonso, and Steven Bass, "401(k) Plan Asset Allocation, Account Balances, and Loan Activity in 2012," Employee Benefit Research Institute, December 2013, http://www.ebri.org/pdf/briefspdf/EBRI_IB_012-13.No394.401k-Update-2012. pdf.

occur regularly and are healthy to the stock and bond markets. It is natural for there to be swings in the daily share prices, and most participants should not be concerned with these movements. In fact, like the occasional rain shower, they can actually be healthy to the markets because they provide growth opportunities for fund managers.

Designing a portfolio for change in the investment climate requires more skill and discipline than designing one for short-term changes. Similar to the economic crashes in 2001 and in 2008, these were climate type of corrections— not only in the stock and bond market, but they also impacted companies, banks, and the economy. If you were an average participant with a significant balance in those years, you felt the pressure to make a significant change in how you invested your money. However, if you were closing in on retirement, it was almost unbearable to watch your account balance lose 20 to 30 percent in value.

Because the date you turn age sixty-five was determined by the day you were born, the only date you can change is the date when you retire! During the economic downturn, many portfolios decreased substantially, to the point where the participants were not able to live off the balance. As a result, many participants panicked and moved their 401(k) balances out of the stock market to low-risk bonds or stable-value accounts. A popular term back then was "My 401(k) turned into a 201(k)!" However, for those who took the longer view and were able to let the market recover, their accounts were rewarded handsomely, with significant returns.

Because the date you turn age sixty-five was determined by the day you were born, the only date you can change is the date when you retire!

This leads me back to my opening statement: When you come out of the stock market is more important than when you get in because you have the ability to pick your gain. If you need to sell your holdings in the short term to borrow from your 401(k) plan for a major purchase, or maybe to begin a retirement income, you will most likely have to accept the market value at that time and the possibility of lower potential returns.

However, a long-term investor, somebody who has a ten-year period to choose when to come out of the market, possibly has more flexibility than someone who is investing for a shorter period of time. If the market is up in the eighth year, the investor could take his money out early. He could give himself a five-year window in which to move his money out of the market and put it in other types of investments. Just like the weather, the stock market is cyclical. A long-term investment strategy makes it easier to benefit from market surges and recover from market declines.

The "Hidden" Risk: Inflation

When people hear the word "risk," they think immediately of the risk that is associated with the daily volatility of the stock market. But there is another risk, a hidden risk that is just as devastating—the risk of inflation. In recent history, inflation has been low, in the 1 to 2 percent range, so people can make a 5 percent return above inflation and still be invested in a fairly conservative portfolio. But when they retire, they do not have the ability to put additional money away, so their portfolio has to be in a position where it can rise above the rate of inflation.

People who start retirement should be aware that inflation can be one of the biggest risks to their retirement security.

Stock-market risk is often built into a portfolio, but there also must be protection against inflation risk. If inflation returns to the level experienced in the early 1980s, 10 to 14 percent, it means that if your money were sitting in a very safe investment like a money-market account, you could lose 10 percent a year because your dollar is worth less at the end of the year than it was at the beginning of the year. People who start retirement should be aware that inflation can be one of the biggest risks to their retirement security.

Interest Rates Impact Bond Value Significantly

As I write this book in 2016, we are at the end of a thirty-year period in which bonds have performed very, very well. A bond investment, unlike stocks, reacts mainly to the interest rate it is paying and the creditworthiness of the company or government that is issuing the bond. A US Government Treasury Bond that pays 6 percent is issued by the US government, so default is unlikely. That type of bond is considered safe. A risk associated with an investment-grade bond is that the interest rate is fixed at the beginning of the term. Very few, if any, 401(k) plans have the ability to buy individual investment-grade bonds, so they must go into a portfolio of bonds. By investing in a bond investment, the portfolio offers a mixture of high- and low-rated bonds, as well as a mixture of high- and low-interest-rate bonds.

A general principle of bond investing is that market interest rates and bond prices typically move in opposite directions. When market interest rates fall, prices of fixed-rate bonds rise.

These portfolios react dramatically to interest-rates moves. If interest rates come down, a bond paying a high interest rate will increase in value. If rates increase, the opposite is true—the value of the bond will decrease in value. It is our fear now, going forward, that if interest rates start to increase, a bond portfolio could actually become the most aggressive and most risky investment for a plan participant. We have been discussing bond risk with employees because most have never seen a period of time when bonds have decreased significantly in value. Most have been working in a period of time when bonds

64

have always been considered safe. As the economy enters a period of rising interest rates, we feel participants should review their holdings and adjust their thinking to accept the new risks associated with bonds—not simply look at past performance to determine their investment selections.

A general principle of bond investing is that market interest rates and bond prices typically move in opposite directions. When market interest rates fall, prices of fixed-rate bonds rise. This phenomenon is known as "interest rate risk." A seesaw is often used to illustrate this concept, as shown below.

Bond Prices and Interest Rates Move in Opposite Directions

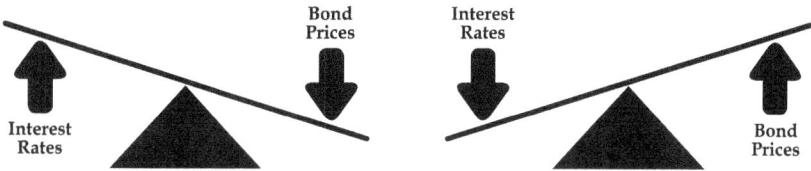

Imagine that one end of the seesaw represents the market interest rate, and the other end represents the price of a fixed-rate bond. As one rises, the other falls.

Market interest rates can have a significant impact on bond prices and values. For example, on a thirty-year government bond paying 6 percent interest, a 1 percent increase in the interest rate could negatively impact the value of that bond by 10 to 15 percent. That is significant.

If the Federal Reserve Board or the bond market itself increases interest rates by 1 percent, a significant number of bond portfolios could suffer substantial negative returns. If interest rates increase 2 percent, it could result in a much higher decrease. It is a matter of mathematics, not predicting the future. The only question becomes *when* it will happen, not *what* will happen to bonds. Historically, as the value of an investment declines, the public will start to liquidate their holdings. When shareholders liquidate, it forces fund managers to liquidate their holdings and causes a strain on their investment strategy. When that happens, more people liquidate, and more money flows out of those funds, causing further declines. Bonds have been in an almost thirty-year period of declining interest rates, causing them to increase in value. We are concerned with what will happen when interest rates start to increase. For that reason, we are being extremely cautious and discussing this phenomenon with our participants who are within ten years of retiring. We feel it is important to make sure they understand bond-related risk and how their investment portfolios could be impacted over the next ten years if interest rates start to increase rapidly.

A Cake Analogy: Investment Options Are Different But Important

To understand the investment options available inside a 401(k) plan, it might be helpful to think about baking a cake. The two most important steps in baking the cake are to use the proper mixture of ingredients and to bake the cake at the proper heat for the correct amount of time. Adding too much of one ingredient would change the taste of the cake significantly, and baking the cake for an insufficient amount of time or for too long also would change the flavor and texture of the cake.

Let's start by visualizing the ingredients in a cake—flour, eggs, butter, vanilla, salt, etc. You can choose to bake a vanilla cake, a strawberry cake, a shortcake, or an angel food cake. The type of cake you end up with is determined by the combination of ingredients you select and the amount of each ingredient used in the recipe. Adding too much salt or vanilla will change the flavor of the cake and could even ruin the cake altogether. Investment options are very similar. To put together a diverse portfolio of investments, you might include investment "ingredients" with US base company stocks; international company stocks; some large-company, dividend-paying stocks; and some smaller-company dividend stocks. Each one of the options you choose is important, and they are important in different combinations. Just like with a cake, too much of one of the funds could cause the portfolio to become unbalanced and change the "investment flavor" and risk level and cause the portfolio to fail to meet your expectations.

So all investment options are not the same, but they are all important in determining the proper portfolio to meet your taste and risk. And the more investment options you have, the more individual "flavors" you can add to your investment cake.

Another key element to baking a cake is how long you leave it in the oven. Just like a cake, if you pull an investment out too soon, or if you leave it in too long, you might experience a less-than-ideal result. If you are a do-it-yourself investor and assemble your own portfolio of investments, it is important that you understand the time you need to let that portfolio stay in the investment "oven," or market, so that it has the perfect opportunity to mature at the right time.

Also, you can make a cake from scratch, go to the store to buy a cake mix in a box, or buy a pre-made cake from a bakery. It's the same with your investment options. Most 401(k) plans offer a wide selection of investment choices for those who wish to make their own "made from scratch" portfolio. There are also the predetermined risk portfolios with all of the ingredients in "the box." The participant can simply select which one meets her needs and would need to determine only when to change the risk level. The last type of choice available is similar to buying a cake pre-made from a store. These options compose the "destination" type portfolios and allow the participant to simply add money. The rest has been done for them!

If we compare our cycling analogy to the cake analogy, the do-it-yourself investor, or unicycle investor is making a cake from scratch. The bicycle investor is using a mix to make a cake. Most of it is done for you; all you have to do is add a cup of oil and a couple eggs, and you have a cake. The third category, the tricycle investor who uses target-date style investments, is buying a cake that someone has already made. All you have to do is pick up the cake and slice it.

The better you understand how stocks, bonds, and cash investments work together in a portfolio, the less of a mystery asset allocation will be, and the better able you will be to optimize the way you invest your money in your 401(k) plan.

Chapter 5 Summary: Key Points to Remember

1. To qualify as offering full diversification, a 401(k) plan can have only three types of investment options: (1) a growth option, which is generally a stock-market investment (stocks); (2) a bond-market investment option, which is a fixed-income option (bonds); or (3) some type of lower risk or fixed-interest option (cash).

2. As you look at the investment options in your 401(k) plan, the most important question to ask yourself is "How much risk am I willing to take between now and the time I will need to start an income stream for retirement?" The more time you have before retirement, the more you can afford the daily volatility of the stock market and the risk associated with it, thereby exposing your account to possible higher yields. And generally, the more stock-market risk you can afford to take, the higher potential rates of return you can get.

3. *Reallocation* is when you change the percentage of assets, or the "allocation," you have invested in those three asset classes (stocks, bonds, cash). We rarely advocate reallocating often—only when your risk level or need for income changes.

4. *Rebalancing* is when you adjust the investment balance in your plan so that your asset-allocation percentages remain consistent and in line with your original choices. We recommend that you rebalance your account at least once a year—quarterly at most.

5. A simple and useful but much-underused tool is the automatic rebalancing feature available in many 401(k) plans. This online tool removes the guesswork out of how and when to rebalance your account.

6. When you get *into* the market is not nearly as important as when you *come out* of the market. A long-term investment strategy makes it easier to benefit from market surges and recover from market declines.

7. Inflation, a "hidden" risk, can be one of the biggest risks to your retirement security. It is critical to build protection against inflation risk into your portfolio to offset the possibility of high inflation during some of your retirement years.

8. A general principle of bond investing is that market interest rates and bond prices typically move in opposite directions. When market interest rates fall, prices of fixed-rate bonds rise. And when rates rise, prices of fixed-rate bonds fall. This phenomenon is known as "interest rate risk."

Understanding Your Plan's Fees

Some of the greatest things in life are free, but unfortunately, a 401(k) plan isn't one of them. You are going to pay a fee for the services and products included in your employer's plan.

Every 401(k) plan has an investment component that is managed by an investment company. It could be a mutual fund company, a bank, an insurance company, or an independent registered investment advisor. They charge a fee to assemble the investment funds to use in the plan and to provide accounting for the plan on a daily basis so that you can check your account balance at the end of the day, either online or by calling an 800 number.

Regardless of who the provider is, some costs are standard with every plan. The investment wrapper is one such cost. It is the technological tool that accounts for everything on a daily basis, including the money that is taken out of your payroll check and deposited into your 401(k) account, your investment earnings, transfers you make, and any loans you might take out against your account. The investment wrapper is sometimes inexpensive and sometimes quite expensive, depending on the options the investment provider offers. Big insurance companies, big mutual funds, and big banks all offer their own types of products and services, including the investment wrapper, web technology, and staff to answer your phone calls when you call in with questions. They also provide due diligence when that money comes in the door; they make sure the right investments are put into the right participants' accounts. That costs money.

A general guideline is that a company—the employer and employees combined—should pay fees equivalent to 1 percent of the plan's asset value in the company's 401(k) plan. Depending on the details of the plan document, an employer will pay some fees, and participants will pay some fees. We have seen employees pay up to 3 percent of plan assets in fees— three times the recommended amount. Paying an additional 1 percent more in fees can cost employees hundreds of thousands of dollars in retirement savings over the span of their careers. It is critical, whether you are an employer or an employee, to understand not just how much you're paying for the plan but exactly what you are paying for.

Large companies such as AT&T negotiate for institutional discounts on investment selections. As a

A general guideline is that a company— the employer and employees combined— should pay fees equivalent to 1 percent of the cost of the company's 401(k) plan.

result, 401(k) participants paid less than half the average 1.4 percent annual expenses charged to all US stock investors, according to a 2013 study from the Investment Company Institute, a Washington-based industry trade group.[31]

By law, employers must manage their 401(k) plans in a way that is in the best interest of their employees. They must ensure that costs are reasonable, offer a diversified investment lineup that performs well, and have the services needed to run the plan effectively.

Fee Disclosure: A Win for Plan Participants

On July 1, 2012, the Department of Labor began requiring 401(k) providers to use a more transparent and standardized approach to disclosing their fees. As part of those new regulations, as of August 31, 2012, 401(k) plan providers also are required to disclose their actual fees to participating employees.[32]

As a result, there is a big push right now to reduce 401(k) plan expenses, or at least to educate plan sponsors and participants about what those expenses are. In general, I am more interested in value than total expenses. Value is what drives our discussions with plan sponsors. Many employers focus on the bottom line and say, "This other company will administer our plan for 10 percent less than you are charging." But they may get 20 percent less value. That less expensive provider might require the employer to go through additional steps to use a certain investment product.

It's sort of like buying a car. Some cars are full luxury models, and others are stripped to the bone. Which one you buy depends on your needs and preferences. Likewise, it's up to the preferences of the employer and employees to determine what kind of investment 401(k) provider they want to use. More features will cost more in fees. Fees are determined by the account value, the size of the plan, the average account balance of the participants, how many deposits they make, how many loans they take out, and how many calls they make to a call center. Every plan has a different fee.

I encourage employers and employees to have an open discussion about what the fees are and negotiate a fair rate. If they want a rock-bottom price, they should expect to receive fewer services. If they want plush options, they should expect—and demand—more services but understand that they will pay more.

A lot of TV shows and news articles discuss how expensive 401(k)s are. In most cases, those reports are driven either by people who want to replace investors' plans with their own or by people who want to promote their cause by selling a book or by advertising a radio or TV news program. People need to pay a fee for the administration of a corporate 401(k) program, but those fees

---

31 John Hechinger, "Retirees Suffer as $300 Billion 401(k) Rollover Boom Enriches Brokers," June 17, 2014, http://www.bloomberg.com/news/2014-06-17/retirees-suffer-as-401-k-rollover-boom-enriches-brokers.html.

32 Stuart Robertson, "Why 401(k) Fee Disclosure Is a Big Win for Small Business Owners," Forbes website, February 10, 2012, http://www.forbes.com/sites/stuartrobertson/2012/02/10/why-401k-fee-disclosure-is-a-big-win-for-small-business-owners/.

should be reasonable. To know what is reasonable, it is important to understand what the fees are for.

Each investment inside of the wrapper has an investment management fee. Also, the third-party administrator and the investment advisor charge fees, as do any trustees who are involved. Each one of these people performs a function. It is important for the employer and employees to understand who is involved in administering a plan, what their fees are, and what they get for those fees. A lot of companies are paying for services and products they never use. So we encourage employers to have open discussions with plan sponsors regarding the fees they are paying and what they get in return. A lot of people who market 401(k) plans say they can provide some services for free, when, in fact, we see very often that fees are hidden or buried. They are just taking a visible fee and turning it into a hard-to-find fee. They still make money, get a commission, and generate revenue for themselves, but they cleverly disguise it.

It is important for the employer and employees to understand who is involved in administering a plan, what their fees are, and what they get for those fees.

With the financial industry heading to a new fiduciary standard, we are seeing a trend in which consumers want more transparency. So hopefully, hidden fees will be a vestige of the past. I also see a trend leading toward more standardization of the product, as well as a more visible "siloing" or division of expenses so that people know exactly what investment providers are charging for.

How to Compare Expenses

It is very difficult for an individual participant to gather the information necessary to analyze plan expenses. Your employer should be working with a rep or advisor who is able to have that discussion and clearly explain all fees. When you are comparing expenses among providers' products, it is not only important to compare how much they are charging—it is important to look also at what they are charging for. A provider who has a robust website and a lot of educational tools may charge slightly more than somebody who has more of a stripped-down version of an investment platform. A good plan is one that offers the options a company's employees are looking for.

How to Change Investments

Eight to ten years ago, the industry went through a period of time where 401(k) participants were doing a lot of market timing inside of their 401(k) plans. They would move into an investment and move out within days. That type of movement generally increases investment expenses in a plan. Most 401(k) investment choices are geared for long-term holdings, not daily trading.

To curb this activity, the US Securities and Exchange Commission issued a

To discourage participants from moving into and investments often, which increases expenses, the SEC allows you to enter and exit the exact same investment only twice in a sixty-day period.

ruling on day trading. It says participants can enter and exit the exact same investment only twice in a sixty-day period. So if you have a growth investment with ABC Company, then in a sixty-day period, you can go in, come out, go in again, and come out. The system will freeze you out of any more movements after that until the next sixty-day period begins.

It is simple to change your investments. You can do so either by making a telephone call or by logging on to your provider's website. A study conducted by a leading 401(k) provider revealed that 80 percent of employees who participate in a 401(k) plan are handling all of the details online. The remaining 20 percent are calling an 800 number and discussing their changes with a live human being.

In the past, it was often the case that old people used the phone and young people used the Internet. That is not true anymore. I have a lot of young people who choose not to use Internet options, and I have a lot of older clients who are robust online users. Today it is more of an access mentality. Either employees are "wired," or they are not. Most of our younger participants want access through their iPhones or other smartphones. As a result, more companies are allowing access through that option.

To ensure that you are paying the least amount possible for the best options, ask your plan provider or employer questions. Find out what you are paying for and what you are getting for the fees you are being charged.

Chapter 6 Summary: Key Points to Remember

1. Some costs are standard with every 401(k) plan. The investment wrapper is one such cost. It is the technological tool that accounts for everything on a daily basis, including the money that is taken out of your payroll check and deposited into your 401(k) account, your investment earnings, transfers you make, and any loans you might take out against your account.

2. A general guideline is that a company—the employer and employees combined—should pay fees equivalent to less than 1 percent of the plan's asset value.

3. On July 1, 2012, the Department of Labor began requiring 401(k) providers to use a more transparent and standardized approach to disclosing their fees. As part of those new regulations, as of August 31,

2012, 401(k) plan providers also are required to disclose their actual fees to participating employees.

4. When you are comparing expenses among providers' products, it is not only important to compare how much they are charging, but it is also important to look at what they are charging for. A provider who has a robust website and a lot of educational tools may charge slightly more than somebody who has more of a stripped-down version of an investment platform. A good plan is one that offers the options a company's employees are looking for.

5. To keep plan participants from moving in and out of their investment options often (called "market timing"), the US Securities and Exchange Commission issued a ruling on day trading. Now participants can enter and exit the exact same investment only twice in a sixty-day period.

6. It is simple to change your investments. You can do so either by making a telephone call or by logging on to your provider's website.

When Retirement Day Comes

Most people retire once in their life, and they're scared to death about doing so. Their decision about when to retire is often based on what they hear at the coffee shop or what they saw their parents or friends do—not on what makes sense for their unique set of circumstances. Retirement is as individual as the participant—every situation is different.

Your Ideal Retirement Age

Today, we think of age sixty-five as the typical retirement age. But that number isn't right for everyone. According to Gallup's annual Economy and Personal Finance survey, conducted in April 2014, the average age at which US retirees report retiring is sixty-two, the highest age Gallup has found since first asking Americans this question in 1991. According to a 2014 Gallup article, "Retirement age may be increasing because many baby boomers are reluctant to retire. Older Americans may also be delaying retirement because of lost savings during the Great Recession or because of insufficient savings even before the economic downturn."[33] Our experience has been that within the past few years, the average retirement age of a retiree from our plans has been increasing substantially. This is driven by two factors: the worker's amount of savings and the worker's health. Balances are down from where they should be, and the health of retirees seems to be much better than when I first started working with retirees thirty years ago.

The first government-adopted retirement age was defined in Germany more than a century ago. In 1889, Germany became the first nation in the world to adopt an old-age social insurance program. Germany's Chancellor, Otto von Bismarck, designed the program and adopted age seventy as the retirement age; he was seventy-four at the time. The idea was first put forward, at Bismarck's suggestion, in 1881 by Germany's Emperor, William the First, in a ground-breaking letter to the German Parliament. William wrote, "Those who are disabled from work by age and invalidity have a well-grounded claim to care from the state." In 1916, the retirement age was lowered to sixty-five.[34]

The thinking was that, at that time, very few people made it to age seventy—and if they did, they deserved a pension. Also, most people didn't live long after that. The United States adapted the system in the 1930s, when we implemented Social Security. The government picked the age of sixty-five for the same reason—that by the time a person working on a farm or in hard labor

---

33 Rebecca Riffkin, "Average US Retirement Age Rises to Sixty-Two," Gallup website, April 28, 2014, http://www.gallup.com/poll/168707/average-retirement-age-rises.aspx.

34 "Age Sixty-Five Retirement," Social Security Administration website, http://www.ssa.gov/history/age65.html.

I ask my clients how they want to retire and at what income they want to retire, not when they want to retire. Age should be a secondary focus.

reached age sixty-five, he was worn out and needed a retirement income. So over the past ninety years or so, we have been using age sixty-five as a retirement date. But that is not the ideal retirement age for everyone; some people retire at a younger age, and some people retire later.

I ask my clients how they want to retire and at what income they want to retire. Age should be a secondary focus. Retirement expert and author Tom Hegna, first mentioned in Chapter 5, talks about two different checks that people get in retirement: "paychecks and playchecks."[35] The goal is to have enough money in retirement to cover your expenses and also to keep doing the things you enjoy. When you retire is a decision that should be based on ensuring the best quality of life after you stop working.

"Normal" and "Early" Retirement

"Normal" retirement and "early" retirement" are both defined in a plan document. The normal retirement age in most plan documents is sixty-five, and early retirement is often set at age fifty-five or sixty. Those ages are simply the age at which the plan document allows people access to their money without any restrictions. But I tell people not to focus on the plan document's wording to determine what "normal" is. You probably have a normal retirement and an early retirement idea in your head, but it is important to work with a financial advisor to determine what is ideal for your situation.

What I consider to be a normal retirement is one that fits the aspirations and dreams of the person who wants to retire. Many people think they should retire at a certain age or a certain income level because that's what everybody else does. But if you make $10,000 at a part-time job that you love and that is physically easy for you to do, that is roughly the equivalent of having an additional $200,000 a year in a 401(k) plan. So if you are going to continue making that income, that's money you can count on to supplement your lifestyle. Each year longer that you continue to work would also reduce the amount needed to fund your retirement income. If we are projecting a lump sum for a couple who needs 30 years of income at age 65, it would be reduced if they work to age 70. This could cut the lump sum need by 15-20 percent for each 5 years they continue to work.

Some people choose to retire from their first job a little bit earlier than is typical. When they're young and healthy, they possibly want to see the world, help their kids a little bit, or help a charity. So they retire early, with

---

35 Tom Hegna is the author of the bestselling book Paychecks and Playchecks: Retirement Solutions for Life (Acanthus Publishing, 2011). He has delivered more than two thousand seminars on his signature Paychecks and Playchecks retirement approach to help Baby Boomers and seniors retire comfortably.

the full intention to come back into a different occupation to finish out the rest of their years. They might retire at age fifty-five, vacation and do the things they want to do for five years, and then go back into the workforce from ages sixty to seventy, knowing that that's what they want to do—not that they have to do it.

Working Past Age Sixty-Five

As stated earlier, we are seeing more and more people work past age sixty-five. It's not always because they have to keep working. Sometimes it is because they want to keep the health insurance and other benefits available to them through the employer. Other people just aren't ready to retire. If you do work past age sixty-five, you can still make contributions to your 401(k) plan, and this might be the time to contribute as much as possible. There is no upper limit on when you can put money into your account. By making the additional contributions, it would allow a couple to reduce their income to an amount similar to what would be available at retirement, basically allowing them to see if they can live on a smaller amount. A lot of people look at those last couple of years as their most important contribution period. If they work another year or two, they might go from being in a position where they can't afford to retire to being able to retire with the type of lifestyle they want.

When Can I Get My Money Out of My 401(k) Plan?

Very few people focus on the distribution phase of a 401(k) plan (getting the money out). Most people focus on the investment phase (putting money in). As you are investing money in your 401(k) plan throughout your career, it is important to consider how you might want to receive the money when you retire—for example, in a lump sum or as a monthly stream of income.

No matter when you choose to retire, you can begin receiving income from your retirement plan any time prior to age 59½ as long as you take your money out in equal and periodic installments. As mentioned in Chapter 3, according to the IRS rule called "72(t)," you can start an income stream if your money is rolled over into an IRA. This rule allows for penalty-free withdrawals from an IRA account, but you must take at least five "substantially equal periodic payments" (SEPPs). The amount depends on your life expectancy calculated with various IRS-approved methods. Penalties apply if you take a distribution from a plan before age 59½, or if you leave the company after age 55.

When you can get your money from your 401(k) plan is a plan provision, but in general, most plans allow for distribution of employee deferrals prior to age 59½, at death, and if you become disabled. (Some plan documents state that employees cannot pull money out prior to age sixty-five.) Although most plans also allow distribution after age 59½ on the deferral (employee) portion, the employer's contributions might be subject to restrictions on access. As an active employee, you could demand the distribution of your contributions and roll them over into an IRA any time after age 59½.

Federal rules state that any employees who have an account balance of more than $5,000 can leave the money in the retirement plan; they are not mandated to do a rollover or take a distribution. Your employer cannot force you out of the plan, even if you retire. If you leave your money in the plan, you can take a lump-sum distribution or a monthly income if permitted by the plan.

Watch Out for Fees

Regardless of how and when you get your money out, the most important question to get answered is "How much does each distribution cost?" A lot of plans charge anywhere from $50 to $100 or more for each distribution.

Regardless of how and when you get your money out, the most important question to get answered is "How much does each distribution cost?" Plans often charge fees ranging from $50 to $100 or more for each distribution. So if you take three distributions a year, you could pay $300 to get your money out for the year. We recommend to most employees that they avoid distribution fees by getting a one-time distribution or setting up a monthly income out of the plan. Roth distributions work the same way and can also be taken out in a lump sum or monthly. Penalties and taxation are completely different for Roth 401(k) plans.

Be Sure to Consider the Tax Implications

It is critical to look at the tax implications of the method you use to take a distribution from the plan.

Again, one reason we recommend using a Roth 401(k) plan is because it is tax-free at retirement. Remember, traditional contributions reduce your taxable income for the current tax year, and the money invested grows tax-deferred until withdrawn at retirement. At retirement, you pay ordinary income tax on all traditional contributions and any growth. In contrast, Roth contributions don't reduce your current taxable income, but there are no taxes on Roth distributions at retirement. You pay taxes up front, and growth is not subject to taxation—at least not according to the current rules.

A lot of people forget to look at the tax implications of their distributions from their 401(k) plan. They can be considerable. Depending on the method used to get your money out to generate an income stream, you could save 15 to 30 percent a year in taxes, giving you more money to live on in retirement.

The hidden trap many retirees forget to check is what we call "bracket jumping." At about $46,000 a year of total adjusted gross income, Social Security starts to become taxable income. Let's say a husband and wife have a household income of $46,000 a year. That means they are in the most favorable income tax bracket. But if their income reaches $60,000 a year, some of their Social Security income will be taxed, increasing the taxes on their entire adjusted gross income. If you were to retire and take a one-time, or lump-sum distribution of $30,000 from your 401(k) plan, that might throw you into a bracket that requires you to pay an additional 20 percent tax on everything. But if you were to pull that $30,000 from a Roth 401(k) instead, it would not be taxable, and it would give you a huge tax savings for that year.

Provisional income amounts if you file as:		
Single, head of household	Married, filing jointly	Then:
Less than **$25,000**	Less than **$32,000**	Social Security income is tax-free
$25,000 to **$34,000**	**$32,000** to **$44,000**	Up to 50% of Social Security income is taxable
More than **$34,000**	More than **$44,000**	Up to 85% of Social Security income is taxable

Build Up Reserves for Emergencies

It happens to all of us. Just when you think you have achieved a healthy balance between monthly expenses and income, something unexpected happens—the car breaks down, the refrigerator quits working, or an adult child needs financial help. We always advise our clients to have money set aside, apart from their retirement savings account, to use when emergencies happen. The same strategy applies once you retire.

Emergencies are one of the biggest retirement burdens many people will endure, and online calculators do not figure emergencies into their calculations. Going into debt to solve an emergency situation is not a good idea; you'll end up paying interest instead of earning it. Using a credit card or savings reserved for normal spending isn't a good idea, either. The best way to be prepared for an emergency is to build up your reserves in advance—a separate stash of money in an account outside of a qualified account like an employer's savings plan, an IRA, or an annuity. That's because if you keep your reserves in that type of plan, and you need emergency funds before you reach the age of 59½, you will incur a tax penalty in addition to normal income tax.

The best way to be prepared for an emergency is to build up your reserves in advance—a separate stash of money in an account outside of a qualified account like an employer's savings plan, an IRA, or an annuity.

79

We recommend that retirees set aside 10 percent of their total investments or one year's worth of spending, whichever number is larger, for reserves.[36]

Retirement day is an event you work toward for decades. Advance preparation is the best tool for ensuring that when the day comes, it gives you reason to celebrate, not panic. Planning for tax implications, investigating fees, and storing up reserves for emergencies can make retirement the happiest time of your life.

Chapter 7 Summary: Key Points to Remember

1. In determining when you should retire, age should be a secondary focus. It is more important to focus on how you want to retire and at what income you want to retire.

2. If you work past age sixty-five, you can still make contributions to your 401(k) plan, and this might be the time to contribute as much as possible. There is no upper age limit on when you can put money into your account.

3. Very few people focus on the distribution phase of a 401(k) plan (getting the money out). Most people focus on the investment phase (putting money in). As you are investing money in your 401(k) plan throughout your career, it is important to consider how you might want to receive the money when you retire—for example, in a lump sum or as a monthly stream of income.

4. No matter when you choose to retire, you can begin receiving income from your retirement plan any time prior to age 59½ as long as you take your money out in equal and periodic installments. Most plans allow for distribution of employee deferrals after age 59½, at death, and if you become disabled.

5. Federal rules state that any employees who have an account balance of more than $5,000 can leave the money in the retirement plan; they are not mandated to do a rollover or take a distribution. Your employer cannot force you out of the plan, even if you retire.

6. Regardless of how and when you get your money out, the most important question to get answered is "How much does each distribution cost?" Plans often charge fees ranging from $50 to $100 or more for each distribution.

---

36 Henry Hebeler, "Online Retirement Calculators Don't Calculate This," MarketWatch.com (The Wall Street Journal) website, July 2, 2014, http://www.marketwatch.com/story/on-line-retirement-calculators-dont-calculate-this-2014-07-02?pagenumber=1.

7. A lot of people forget to look at the tax implications of their distributions from their 401(k) plan. A hidden trap many retirees forget to check is what we call "bracket jumping." This term refers to the income threshold that puts you into a new tax bracket, one that could require you to pay additional taxes. If you were to retire and take a one-time, or lump-sum distribution, that might throw you into a bracket that requires you to pay an additional 20 percent tax on everything. But if you were to pull that money from a Roth 401(k) instead, it would not be taxable, and it would give you a huge tax savings for that year.

8. Emergencies are one of the biggest retirement burdens many people will endure, and online calculators do not figure emergencies into their calculations. The best way to be prepared for an emergency is to build up your reserves in advance—a separate stash of money in an account outside of a qualified account like an employer's savings plan, an IRA, or an annuity.

Creative 401(k) Strategy:
Getting the Most Out of Your Plan

If you have access to a 401(k) plan through your employer and you are contributing to it, you are way ahead of many Americans, in terms of saving for retirement. According to the Bureau of Labor Statistics, only about 55 percent of the American workforce has access to a 401(k), and only about 38 percent participate.[37]

However, if you are not well informed about how to maximize your long-term savings in your plan—and if you do not actively monitor and optimize the way your plan is working for you—you could be losing a lot of money in potential future savings. Too many people put in a minimum contribution they can afford and not what they need to save. They pick an initial investment strategy and never look again to make sure it's the right portfolio for their age, risk status, and life stage. As a result, they limp along with that ill-suited plan for the next thirty years and expect to retire off of whatever they've accumulated. They fail to realize that small changes make huge differences.

Here are some steps you can take to get the most out of your 401(k) plan:

1. Take advantage of the age-based portfolios that help people invest. These represent a big step forward for participants in 401(k) plans by simplifying one of their hardest choices—investment selection.

2. Study current trends and try to find strategies that work for you. Some of those strategies are not new; they're just general investment strategies. Learn everything you can about all of your investment options and the risks and potential rewards associated with each one.

3. Make sure your account is fully diversified. Instead of selecting only US-based investment options, take advantage of all of the asset classes. Most plans offer twenty to thirty options or more, and they include all of the traditional asset classes. Some also include real estate investments and commodities investments. Consider a truly diversified portfolio, including US-based growth and value investment styles, international, and commodity asset classes, for example, unless you have selected an age-based portfolio.

---

37 Elizabeth MacBride, "The Right Ways to Get Workers Hooked on a 401(k)," March 7, 2014, CNBC website, http://www.cnbc.com/id/101469896.

4. Save a little more than you are currently saving. Over a thirty-year period, adding 2 to 3 percent of your salary into your account can add hundreds of thousands of dollars to your account by the time you reach the age of sixty-five. Try to contribute the maximum amount of money allowed by law into your account. That limit is $18,000 in 2016 and $24,000 for people over the age of fifty-five. If you can't hit these amounts, start small but increase often.

5. Increase your contributions if you receive an unexpected windfall of money from an inheritance. You cannot deposit an unexpected windfall into your 401(k) account as a lump sum. But what you can do is increase your contributions from your paycheck until you reach the maximum, and use the money you received to live on. For example, let's say you make $50,000 a year at your job, and you are currently putting 6 percent of your salary into your 401(k) account, which is $3,000 per year. One day, you find out that your Uncle Sid has left you an inheritance of $30,000. You can increase your deferrals to the full $18,000, which is 35 percent of your salary, and live off of your inheritance from Uncle Sid until it runs out. Then you can adjust your deferral back down to 6 percent of your salary, or the maximum amount you can afford to contribute. This is the way to get the maximum out of the plan and all of the tax advantages that go along with it.

6. If you are married, find ways to maximize both your and your spouse's deferral contributions. Examine the differences between the two plans to see which one has the better investment options and the better employer match. If your plan has a dollar-for-dollar match of up to 6 percent, and your spouse's plan has a company matching contribution, put as much money as possible into your own plan to get the biggest employer contribution. That makes more sense than putting 3 percent of pay into your account and 3 percent of pay in your spouse's account.

If you're thinking that all of that sounds difficult, you are not alone. Making the most of your 401(k) is not for the weak at heart. If you do not understand the process, I strongly recommend that you seek the help of a financial advisor who can guide you. The fees you will pay that person could pale in comparison to the tens or hundreds of thousands of additional dollars you can get out of your plan during your working years.

By doing a little bit of research, talking with people who are experienced in investment strategies, and seeking out guidance to help you find out how to add a little more return to your portfolio, you can end up with a lot of additional cash in your 401(k) plan by the time you retire. That is the way to work smarter instead of harder. To get a comparable increase in retirement savings without optimizing your 401(k) plan, you would have to work a lot of overtime and save that money—and that still wouldn't get you even close to the additional returns you could possibly achieve in a 401(k) plan over time.

Don't just accept your basic plan as it looks when you first begin contributing. It's like driving a car or researching a family vacation—it takes some effort to make it work for you. If people would put the same amount of resources and time into optimizing their lifetime savings as they do into planning a vacation, they could add significant amounts of extra performance. It is especially important for you to diversify and look further than just one or two investment options, especially if you have more than $10,000 in your 401(k) account. (Using diversification as part of your investment strategy neither assures nor guarantees better performance and cannot protect against loss of principal due to changing market conditions.)

How Life Insurance Fits into Your Plan

Today, fewer 401(k) plans allow participants to purchase life insurance as an investment selection in their plan. Many of the large plans have provisions that do not allow for the purchase of life insurance, but a lot of the smaller plans, such as those that are offered through independent third-party administrators (TPAs) and some of the insurance-company-based providers, do allow for the purchase of life insurance. If your plan allows this option, it can be a great way for you to buy life insurance on a tax-favored basis. Basically, you are allowed to use up to 25 percent of your contribution toward the premiums to purchase a universal life or term policy or 50 percent of your contribution toward the purchase of a whole life policy.

Those who are contributing substantial amounts of money into a 401(k) can get anywhere from $100,000 to $2 million of coverage using tax-deductible contributions to pay their premiums. Those with large account balances from rollovers who have been participants in a plan for longer than five years can use all of their account balance—100 percent of it—toward the purchase of life insurance. Depending on your age and health, you could buy $4 million to $7 million worth of coverage with your 401(k) balance.

If your 401(k) plan allows you to purchase life insurance as part of the plan, it is an excellent way to obtain life insurance on a very tax-favored basis.

For people who have large life insurance needs, and a plan that allows for it, the life insurance purchase may make sense because the death benefit comes out free of federal income taxes when the participant dies. In exchange for this income tax-free death benefit, the government collects a small amount of income tax each year, which is often lower than an equivalent term policy premium. This is often a sensible way to get a significant amount of extra coverage on a very tax-favored basis. However, the death benefits may be subject to federal estate and state inheritance taxes. Please consult a qualified advisor for details on your specific needs.

Buying life insurance through a 401(k) plan is a complicated procedure. It requires that you investigate the plan document and your individual situation thoroughly. It is best to consult an advisor or call our firm to get more information. I have spoken throughout the United States on this topic and have worked with other advisors to help their clients maximize this unique approach.

This strategy does not make sense if you plan to leave your employer soon. If you have to move the policy out, you could suffer substantial contractual penalties in the life insurance. Buying life insurance this way also is not an ideal strategy for people who have small account balances (less than $50,000). They need to focus on getting the most money possible into a stock-market type of investment to build up their retirement savings. Most plan documents provide an exclusion that says anyone who has less than $50,000 cannot purchase life insurance.

Not only can you purchase life insurance on yourself as a participant, but the rules in most documents allow you to purchase life insurance on anybody you have an insurable interest in. For example, a business owner can purchase coverage on his partner. A husband can purchase coverage on his wife, a child, or a parent. You also can purchase "second to die" coverage, which is a policy used specifically to pay estate taxes. This option solves many problems at the same time.

If your 40(k) plan does not allow you to purchase life insurance, consider buying it on your own, as a supplement to your retirement savings plan. It is an important part of any financial plan, especially if you have dependents.

Sustainable Investment Strategy™

Disclaimer: Mutual funds are sold by prospectus only. Before investing, investors should carefully consider the investment objectives, risks, charges, and expenses of a mutual fund. The fund prospectus provides this and other important information. Please contact your representative or the Company to obtain a prospectus. Please read the prospectus carefully before investing or sending money.

Variable annuities are long-term investments suitable for retirement funding and are subject to market fluctuations and investment risk, including the possibility of loss of principal. Variable annuities are sold by prospectus, which contains information about the variable annuity, including a description of applicable fees and charges. These include, but are not limited to, mortality and expense risk charges, administrative fees, and charges for optional benefits and riders. The prospectus can be obtained from the insurance company offering the variable annuity or from your financial professional. Read it carefully before you invest.

An investment in the Money Market Fund is not insured or

86

guaranteed by the Federal Deposit Insurance Corporation or any other government agency. Although the Fund seeks to preserve the value of your investment at $1.00 per share, it is possible to lose money by investing in the Fund.

Investors should consider carefully information contained in the prospectus, including investment objectives, risks, charges, and expenses. Please read the prospectus carefully before investing. ETFs do not sell individual shares directly to investors and issue their shares only in large blocks. Exchange-traded funds are subject to risks similar to those of stocks. Investment returns will fluctuate and are subject to market volatility so that an investor's shares, when redeemed or sold, may be worth more or less than their original cost.

When you retire, you don't want a basket of money; you want a steady income stream to last you throughout your retirement. Financial Solutions Midwest's Sustainable Income Strategy™ (SIS™) provides a continuous "cycle" to help you achieve your goals. Many of the pensions we advise use this concept, and it is not new. The strategy divides your retirement savings into six segments, or "baskets," each intended to provide five years of income. Thus, the six baskets provide a total of thirty years of retirement income. They contain a mix of conservative and aggressive investments.

This strategy helps ensure that you get the most out of your 401(k) plan when you retire. We devised this concept to give us a visual way to explain to clients how we can help them achieve their lifelong goals in a more efficient manner. We live in a farming community, so we wanted to come up with six baskets showing the different stages in the growth cycle. The idea is to avoid eating all of your "fruit" at once and to ensure that you have other "food" growing behind the food you are harvesting now, as well as some left over to seed future income. In other words, this concept helps you maintain a balance of currently available assets while also investing for the future.

Because SIS™ is based on a continuous cycle of fixed-income and long-term investments, it can help you reach your goals in retirement, ensure that your necessary expenses are covered, and allow you to maintain your current lifestyle. Not only that—you could also possibly get regularly scheduled income payment increases to help protect you against rising costs.

SIS™ illustrates how to turn an asset into an income stream and have peace of mind knowing there is a

Financial Solutions Midwest's Sustainable Investment Strategy™ divides your retirement years into six "baskets" to help you maintain a balance of currently available assets while also investing for the future.

five-year reserve of income in case the portfolio and the market go down. It is also easy to understand and gives us a unique way to look at asset allocation. (Please note that using asset allocation as part of your investment strategy neither assures nor guarantees better performance and cannot protect against loss of principal due to changing market conditions.)

Here is how the six "baskets" are invested:

Basket #1: The first basket is invested in the most secure and liquid options for the first five years of distribution. We use various investments with little or no risk like CDs or money market investments. For example, if you need $20,000 a year for five years, we allocate about $93,000. We assume a rate of interest that tells us how much money you need in the first basket.

Basket #2: The second basket is invested a little bit more aggressively because you wouldn't need it for five years, since we are taking 100 percent of the income from the first basket. We assume a higher interest rate in this basket, which takes the distribution from years five through ten. Investments at this stage become a little bit less liquid and a little more risky. Bond and bank-rate-based investments and fixed annuities would possibly fill this basket.

Basket #3: The third basket invests even a little bit more aggressively, so we're looking at more of a balanced approach between stocks and bonds or stocks and other fixed-interest investments. This basket takes your income distributions from the tenth year to the fifteenth year. Our main objective here is to have a mixture of investments that could receive some market gains with other investments, striving to preserve principle.

Baskets #4–#6: For the fourth, fifth, and sixth baskets, we use an interest assumption to come up with the amount of money you need to invest during those years so that the income stream will sustain you for thirty years. In effect, these three baskets can be invested aggressively because you will not need them soon.

The following chart shows important features of the six baskets. The key is to realize that at the end of each five-year period, the portfolio is reallocated to the lower basket. The portfolio gets more conservative as time goes on and each "basket" is depleted:

Basket	Features	Bottom Line
1	• This is one of two baskets providing a fixed income. • Covers years 1–5 of retirement. • Product options include cash, money market, or CDs. • Is very liquid, low yielding.	This basket contains cash and equivalents. This is your liquid money. Use it for income in the first five years of retirement.
2	• This is the second of two baskets providing a fixed income. • Covers years 6–10 of retirement. • Liquidate in year 5 and invest in Basket 1. • Product options include fixed annuity or fixed income. • Provides stable value with moderate liquidity.	The fixed-income investments in Basket 2 last for intermediate duration and produce higher yields than money market and short-term bonds.
3	• It contains a moderate portfolio of equity investments. • Covers years 11–15 of retirement. • Product options include moderately conservative investment strategies. • Provides some equity exposure with contractual income benefits.	Includes income protection investments with a balance of conservative equities.
4	• This is a balanced portfolio of equity investments. • Covers years 16–20 of retirement. • Product options include moderately aggressive investment strategies. • Provides some equity exposure with contractual income benefits.	This basket is reserved for investment protectors instead of income protectors. We want to make sure our clients can get their money back at the end of the term, regardless of market performance.
5	• This is an aggressive portfolio of equity investments. • Covers years 21–25 of retirement. • Liquidate at end of year 20.	Includes mostly equities and professionally managed accounts.

Basket	Features	Bottom Line
6	• This is an equity-aggressive portfolio of investments. • Covers years 26–30 of retirement. • Product options include equities offered through exchange-traded funds or individual stock portfolios.	This basket holds the most aggressive assets. The money is expected to be used for a maximum of twenty-five years, in most instances.

A more detailed diagram of the basket strategy is included in the Appendix.

Most people tend to make wise, informed, educated choices about their education, career, marriage, parenting, home purchases, and other major life decisions. But too few people apply that same diligence to getting the most out of their 401(k) plan. Yet it is, by far, the most important aspect of financial health in a person's lifetime. We encourage you to do everything you can to optimize the decisions you make about the contribution, investment, and distribution phases of your retirement planning.

Chapter 8 Summary: Key Points to Remember

1. Small changes can make a big difference in the amount of money you have in your retirement account by the time you retire. By doing a little bit of research, talking with people who are experienced in investment strategies, and seeking out guidance to help you find out how to add a little more return to your portfolio, you can end up with a lot of additional cash in your 401(k) plan by the time you retire.

2. Today, fewer 401(k) plans allow participants to purchase life insurance as an investment selection in their plan. Many of the large plans have provisions that do not allow for the purchase of life insurance, but a lot of the smaller plans, such as those that are offered through independent third-party administrators (TPAs) and some of the insurance-company-based providers, do allow for the purchase of life insurance. If your plan allows this option, it can be a great way for you to buy life insurance on a tax-favored basis. Basically, you are allowed to use up to 25 percent of your contribution toward the premiums to purchase a universal life or term policy or 50 percent of your contribution toward the purchase of a whole life policy.

3. If your 40(k) plan does not allow you to purchase life insurance, consider buying it on your own, as a supplement to your retirement

savings plan. It is an important part of any financial plan, especially if you have dependents.

4. When you retire, you don't want a basket of money; you want a steady income stream to last you throughout your retirement. Financial Solutions Midwest's Sustainable Income Strategy™ (SIS™) provides a continuous "cycle" to help you achieve your goals. This concept is not new, but our method of calculating the investments over time is unique. This strategy divides your retirement savings into six segments, or "baskets," each intended to provide five years of income. Thus, the six baskets provide a total of thirty years of retirement income. They contain a mix of conservative and aggressive investments.

I'm Retired—Now What?

After all those years—decades—of having your deferrals taken out of your paycheck and placed in your retirement account, now you have finally retired. This is unfamiliar territory for most retirees.

I have talked with many 401(k) participants and investment advisory clients who come into my office with a blank stare in their eyes once they are ready to retire. They have accumulated a nice amount of money but are completely bewildered about what to do next. The comment that comes next varies somewhat but basically goes like this: "I have worked my entire life as an engineer [or doctor or successful business owner]. I have been doing a pretty good job of saving the money, and I have been doing a great job of investing the money while it's in the market. But nobody has ever taught me how to invest money for an income."

It is absolutely critical that few mistakes are made in the distribution phase of your 401(k) plan. Withdrawals and lump-sum allocations all have significant long-term impacts on the total performance of the plan.

Figuring out what to do with your money once you reach retirement is an extremely complicated process. I strongly recommend that you seek the guidance of a financial advisor who is looking out for your interests. He or she can help you sort through all of your options.

It is absolutely critical that few mistakes are made in the distribution phase of your 401(k) plan. Taking too much out in a downturn, making an incorrect allocation when money is needed, taking lump-sum withdrawals to buy vehicles or other purchases immediately after retirement—all have significant long-term impacts on the total performance of the plan.

What to Do with Your Money Once You Retire

The answer to the question "What should I do with my money now?" is specific to each retiree's situation. As mentioned, taxes can have a massive impact on an individual's account balance and withdrawal rate. Be sure to consider tax ramifications when taking a retirement income.

Rollover Considerations

Before rolling assets over from a qualified plan, you should consider various factors, including but not limited to the following:

- **Investment options**—An IRA often enables the investor to select from a broader range of investment options.

- **Fees and expenses**—Both plans involve investment-related expenses and plan or account fees. IRA fees may be more than your current plan fees.

- **Services**—Different levels of service may be available under each option.

- **Penalty-free withdrawals**—It may be easier to borrow from a plan, and you may be able to withdraw funds earlier in certain circumstances.

- **Required minimum distributions**—If you are still working at 70½, you generally are not required to make distributions from an employer's plan.

- **Tax considerations**—To determine potential tax considerations, consult with your tax advisor.

Additional factors may be relevant when analyzing considerations that might apply to your specific circumstances. Consult your financial professional.

Your Three Options

Once you retire, you have basically three options: You can leave your money inside the 401(k) plan, roll it over tax-free into an IRA, or simply cash in the account and pay the taxes.

If your account balance contains less than $5,000, the rules that govern retirement plans mandate that you cannot be required to remove your money. You have the option of taking a monthly income, a quarterly distribution, or an annual distribution from your 401(k) plan. Many plans permit only lump-sum payments.

If you roll your money over into an IRA, you can do so without incurring federal income taxes, so no income tax is due at the time of the rollover. You can postpone paying the taxes until you start taking an income stream from the IRA. And once your money is in an IRA, you have a lot more latitude of investment choices. If you leave it in the 401(k) plan, you will be limited by the investment choices offered in the plan, but if you move it into an IRA, you can invest in a wider variety of investment choices. The fees may be higher with IRAs, however.

You will have more investment options with an IRA than with a 401(k) plan, but the fees associated with an IRA are often higher than they are with a 401(k) plan.

Americans shifted $321 billion from 401(k)s and similar plans to IRAs in 2012, up about 60 percent in the past decade, according to financial-services research firm Cerulli Associates.[38]

If you plan to use your 401(k) money for casual distributions from time to time, then leaving it inside of the 401(k) plan may be

---

38 John Hechinger, "Brokers Take Rollovers for a Ride," Bloomberg Businessweek website, June 19, 2014, http://www.businessweek.com/articles/2014-06-19/brokers-401-k-rollover-pitches-can-be-dodgy.

the best option. But if you don't have the amount of money you need to meet your income goal and you need to build more income guarantees around that income stream, then rolling it into an IRA may be the better option. Again, this is an individual solution that should be based on your unique needs. It is tough to make a generalization about which option is better.

When a doctor recommends a medicine for you, your decision about whether to follow his advice is largely based on that doctor's professionalism and how much you trust him. That should be the case with your retirement savings, too. Seek out quality advice from an advisor you trust.

Government Oversight of IRA Rollovers

Right now, there is a lot of government scrutiny about the appropriateness of rolling over retirees' money into IRAs. Some circles of opinion in the government claim that it might be a breach of fiduciary duty for a financial advisor to recommend an IRA rollover and make a commission as a result.

The US Department of Labor proposed rules that brokers and other advisors act in clients' best interests during rollovers, a so-called "fiduciary standard." Brokers are generally held to the different standard of selling products that are suitable for their customers, meaning they don't have to put their clients' interests first as long as they select appropriate investments.[39] This may not mean they are less interested in what is best for you; it simply means they can make product choices that pay commissions.

Pay Attention to the Required Minimum Distribution

The required minimum distribution (RMD) is the topic *du jour* of anybody who is older than sixty-five because they hear rumors in the coffee shop and other places about penalties for failing to get the RMD correct. The penalties for not getting the minimum distribution correct are indeed substantial.

In general, you can expect that your RMD will equal about 3 percent of your account balance at age 70½. For example, if you have a $200,000 account balance when you retire, your annual RMD would be roughly 3 percent of that amount, or $6,000.

However, if you continue to work after age 70½ and are not in the highly compensated class of employees, you may defer your RMD until you quit working for that employer who sponsors the plan. If you have other 401(k) accounts and do not work for that employer, you will need to satisfy the RMD requirement as well unless it is combined with a 401(k) plan where you are currently working.

Age 70½ Is when RMDs Must Begin if You Are Retired

You cannot keep retirement funds in your account indefinitely. You generally are required to start taking withdrawals from your traditional IRA or 401(k) retirement plan account when you reach age 70½ (six calendar months after

---

39 Ibid.

your seventieth birthday). For example, if you turn 70½ in 2016, you will be required to take a distribution by the end of 2017.

Roth IRAs do not require withdrawals until after the death of the owner, however. In other words, RMDs do not apply to Roth IRA or Roth 401(k) plans. (Beneficiaries of Roth plans do have to comply with RMD rules, however.)

Your RMD is the minimum amount you must withdraw from your account each year. In general, your age, the age of your spouse if living, and account value determine the amount you must withdraw. You can always take out more than the minimum required amount if you choose to. Your withdrawals will be included in your taxable income except for any part that was already taxed or any part that can be received tax-free (such as qualified distributions from designated Roth accounts).

Once you turn 70½, you must begin to take a required minimum distribution (RMD) from your traditional 401(k) plan or Roth IRA, which will be roughly 3 percent of your account balance.

According to the IRS, the RMD for any year is the account balance as of the end of the immediately preceding calendar year divided by a distribution period from the IRS's "Uniform Lifetime Table." A separate table is used if the sole beneficiary is the owner's spouse who is ten or more years younger than the owner.

The RMD applies equally to any money that is in "qualified status," which means a qualified IRA, a qualified 401(k), or another qualified retirement plan.

The first year following the year you reach age 70½, you will generally have two required distribution dates: an April 1 withdrawal (for the year you turn 70½) and an additional withdrawal by December 31 (for the year following the year you turn 70½). To avoid having both of these amounts included in your income for the same year, you can make your first withdrawal by December 31 of the year you turn 70½ instead of waiting until April 1 of the following year.

For each subsequent year after your required beginning date, you must withdraw your RMD by December 31. If you are unable to take your minimum distribution in the calendar year in which you are required to take a distribution, there is a provision that gives you a little leeway. You have until the time you file your income taxes (through April 15th of the next year) to make that first distribution. However, that means you will end up taking two distributions in that year: one for the year prior and one for the current year. As a result, your taxable distribution will be doubled for that year.

Married vs. Single

The formulas for single and married people are different. If you are single, the minimum distribution is based on your age. If you are married, it is based on the average age of you and your spouse.

On FINRA's website (http://apps.finra.org/Calcs/1/RMD) is an interactive

95

RMD calculator. Plan participants whose primary beneficiary is a spouse more than ten years younger must use the Joint Life Expectancy Table in IRS Publication 590, which will generally produce lower required distributions.

If You Have Multiple IRAs

If you have more than one IRA, you must calculate the required minimum distribution for each IRA separately each year. But you do not have to take a distribution from every account; you can aggregate your RMD amounts for all of your IRAs and withdraw the total from one IRA.

This is an important point to note for retirees: If you have more than one IRA, you must calculate the RMD for each IRA separately each year. However, you may aggregate your RMD amounts for all of your IRAs and withdraw the total from one of the IRAs, not each individual IRA. RMDs for qualified plan accounts other than IRAs must be calculated and paid separately from the RMDs for your IRAs. If you have more than one qualified retirement plan account, the RMD must be calculated and paid separately for each qualified plan or 401(k) account.

Many retirees are confused by this requirement. They think they have to take (not just calculate) a required minimum distribution from each IRA they own. If a retiree has three different brokers or uses three different banks for her IRAs, she will receive notices about three different required minimum distributions. For fear of being penalized for noncompliance, she might withdraw money from all three.

This is where help from an advisor can benefit you. For our clients, we set up schedules of minimum distribution and then place them on a calendar so that we can make sure our clients are meeting their minimum distributions and taking the money from the right accounts. If a retiree has an IRA that is underperforming, we may choose to take the entire distribution from that IRA. On the other hand, if she has an IRA that is performing very well over the long term, we may choose never to pull a distribution out of that one and let the money accumulate because it is achieving good growth.

Unfortunately, this is a manual process for 401(k) plans, and the RMD has to be updated each year. Depending on in the 401(k), the RMD is often determined by the investment provider or the third-party administrator, the TPA firm. But in the case of an IRA, it is often set up automatically. If you have an IRA through an investment company or a bank, you can sign a form asking for your required minimum distributions to be deducted automatically.

It is beneficial for retirees to consolidate all of their retirement accounts into one. We recommend that retirees roll their IRAs into their 401(k) plan or roll all of their accounts into one IRA. If they choose not to do that, we recommend that they at least maintain all of their accounts with one advisor so that he or she can control the process easily. Mistakes are less likely to occur if one person is handling all of an investor's accounts. Having all of your retirement savings together also makes it a lot easier to successfully manage your money in your retirement years and to manage your required distribution.

Missing the RMD Deadline Will Cost You

If you do not take any distributions, or if the distributions are not large enough, you may have to pay a 50 percent excise tax on the amount that was not distributed as required. For example, if your RMD is $10,000 and you don't withdraw that amount by the end of the year, the penalty will be $5,000 plus income tax. To report the excise tax, you may have to file IRS Form 5329, "Additional Taxes on Qualified Plans (Including IRAs) and Other Tax-Favored Accounts."

Investment providers are often held responsible if a retiree misses the RMD deadline, even though they notify their client of the deadline. Clients often get angry if they miss a distribution and will move their money somewhere else. That is why most providers are diligent about making sure the distributions are handled properly.

What Happens when a Plan Participant Dies

All 401(k) plans and IRAs contain a beneficiary designation. It is usually the most overlooked designation, and mistakes can have a huge tax impact on the account. For that reason, when our clients go into retirement, we strongly encourage them to update all of their beneficiary forms to make adjustments for children or spouses who have died or to make changes in where they want their money to go when they die. Often, people want to incorporate a charity into their portion of their retirement plan, which gives them the benefit of getting some tax breaks on the distribution. It is important to make sure your beneficiary designation is correct.

The beneficiary designation within all 401(k) plans and IRAs is usually the most overlooked designation, and mistakes can create a huge tax impact on the account.

We have seen disastrous results when plan participants fail to ensure that their beneficiary forms are correct. A lot of people don't realize that if your last will and testament designates one person as the beneficiary and your 401(k) and/or IRA designates someone else, the 401(k) and IRA will supersede your will.

We could write an entire chapter on a discussion about how many generations you can keep an IRA or a 401(k) plan going. The biggest differentiator you need to be aware of is that in a 401(k) plan, under the provisions of the document, the money is available only for the participant and the spouse or one beneficiary. There is limited ability for 401(k) plans to provide distributions for multiple generations. In contrast, IRAs allow owners to stipulate that the money will go to not only the spouse but also the children and grandchildren. The owner can set up a required minimum distribution strategy that can stretch as long as forty or fifty years after he dies. It's one of the biggest benefits of an IRA over a traditional 401(k) plan.

Another difference to consider is that, after the death of a participant, if the spouse dies after the participant does, the 401(k) plan mandates a distribution and immediate taxability.

Making wise decisions is critical during the *investment* phase, when you are contributing money into your 401(k) plan and choosing the right mix of investments. It is just as critical that you make prudent decisions during the *distribution* phase, when you are using your 401(k) plan to fund your retirement. Regardless of which phase you are in, consulting with a trusted advisor can help you avoid costly mistakes. Knowing as much as possible about your options, limitations, and government regulations can save you tens or hundreds of thousands of dollars in the long run. The more you educate yourself now, the more money you will have when you retire.

It is important to always keep your beneficiary designation current and up to date.

Chapter 9 Summary: Key Points to Remember

1. It is absolutely critical that few mistakes are made in the distribution phase of your 401(k) plan. Taking too much out in a downturn, making an incorrect allocation when money is needed, taking lump-sum withdrawals to buy vehicles or other purchases immediately after retirement—all have significant long-term impacts on the total performance of the plan.

2. The answer to the question "What should I do with my money now?" is specific to each retiree's situation. Be sure to consider tax ramifications when taking a retirement income.

3. Once you retire, you have basically three options: You can leave your money inside the 401(k) plan, roll it over tax-free into an IRA, or simply cash in the account and pay the taxes.

4. Your required minimum distribution (RMD) is the minimum amount you must withdraw from your account each year. In general, your age, the age of your spouse if living, and account value determine the amount you must withdraw.

5. You generally are required to start taking withdrawals from your traditional IRA or 401(k) retirement plan account when you reach age 70½. Roth IRAs do not require withdrawals until after the death of the

owner, however. In other words, RMDs do not apply to Roth IRA or Roth 401(k) plans.

6. The penalties for not getting the RMD correct are substantial. Also, if you do not take any distributions, or if the distributions are not large enough, you may have to pay a 50 percent excise tax on the amount that was not distributed as required.

7. In general, you can expect that your RMD will equal about 3 percent of your account balance at age 70½.

8. All 401(k) plans and IRAs contain a beneficiary designation. It is usually the most overlooked designation, and mistakes can have a huge tax impact on the account. If your last will and testament designates one person as the beneficiary and your 401(k) and/or IRA designates someone else, the 401(k) and IRA will supersede your will.

9. In a 401(k) plan, under the provisions of the document, the money is available only for the participant and the spouse or one beneficiary. There is limited ability for 401(k) plans to provide distributions for multiple generations. In contrast, IRAs allow owners to stipulate that the money will go to not only the spouse but also the children and grandchildren.

10. Keep your beneficiary designation up-to-date!

Appendix

Supporting Document for Chapter 1

Are You on Target to Retire?

Desired Monthly Income for 25 years				
Distribution Rate	$3,000	$4,000	$5,000	$6,000
Lump Sum Needed @ 4%	$568,357	$757,809	$947,262	$1,136,715
Lump Sum Needed @ 5%	$513,180	**$684,240**	$855,300	$1,026,360
Lump Sum Needed @ 6%	$465,620	$620,827	$776,034	$931,241

How Much Do I Need to Save Monthly to Accumulate $684,240?

Years to Retirement	45 w/ no savings	35 w/ no savings	25 w/ no savings	15 w/ no savings
Interest earned @ 8%	$130	$298	$719	$1,977
Interest earned @ 10%	$65	$180	$515	$1,650
Interest earned @ 12%	$32	$106	$364	$1,369

Years to Retirement	45 w/ no savings	35 w/ $15,000 savings	25 w/ $50,000 savings	15 w/ $100,000 savings
Interest earned @ 8%	$130	$192	$334	$1,022
Interest earned @ 10%	$65	$51	$61	$576
Interest earned @ 12%	$32	---	---	$169

This is for illustrative purposes only. Hypothetical interest is assumed. Performance is not guaranteed.

For more information on retirement planning, contact Brian D. Heckert, CLU, ChFC, QPFC, Financial Solutions Midwest, 618-327-3267.

Supporting Documents for Chapter 2

Retirement Plan Comparison Grid

Savings for Retirement 401(k) vs. Roth IRA vs. Taxable Account

Inputs:

Annual contribution: $2,400

Years until retirement: 25

Anticipated annual rate of return: 8%

Long-term captial gains tax rate: 15%

Ordinary income tax rate: 20%

Percent of Earnings that is Long-Term: %70

Percent of earnings that is qualified dividends: 30%

Long-term gains recognizedper year: 20%

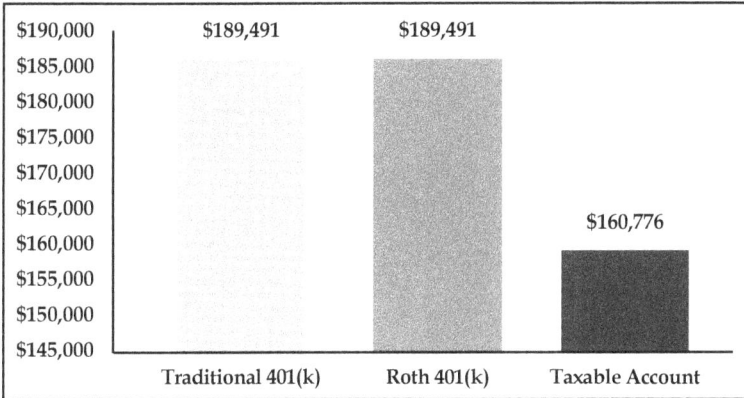

Bar chart comparing values: Traditional 401(k) $189,491, Roth 401(k) $189,491, Taxable Account $160,776.

Summary

Contributions of $60,000 to a taxable account will yield you approximately $5,631 per year in retirement because you would have to pay long-term gains on distributions above your cost basis. In comparison, a 4 percent distribution rate from your Roth 401(k) will yield you approximately $7,578 in retirement because you pay no taxes upon withdrawals. If you choose to have your funds invested in a traditional IRA, your 4 percent distribution would yield you approximately $6,064. For a traditional IRA, you would pay ordinary income taxes on all withdrawals.

Below is a deeper comparison of the two types of accounts that may yield you the most in retirement.

Comparative Results	Traditional 401(k)	Roth 401(k)
Total of Contributions	$60,000.00	$60,000.00
Balance at Retirement	$189,490.60	$189,490.60
Taxes Due for Distributions	-$37,898.12	$0.00
Value of Invested Tax Savings	$29,650.81	$0.00
Net Withdrawal at Retirement	$181,243.29	$189,490.60
Net Comparison	**-$8,247.31**	**$8,247.31**

Investment Risk Assessment Profile

How should I allocate my assets? More than 90 percent of investment returns are determined by how investors allocate their assets versus security selection, market timing and other factors.[40] Review the following questions to become familiar with our Risk Analyzer found on our website below. For a complete Risk Analysis assessment, visit: www.financialsolutionsmidwest.com/library/calculators. See the "Investments" Section: What is my risk tolerance?

Attitudes toward Risk

1. What is your age?
   A) 35 years or under
   B) 36–54
   C) 55 or above

2. What do you expect to be your next major expenditure?
   A) Buying a house
   B) Paying for a college education
   C) Capitalizing a new business
   D) Providing for retirement

3. When do you expect to use most of the money you are now accumulating in your investments?
   A) At any time now...so a high level of liquidity is important
   B) Probably in the future...25 years from now
   C) In 6–10 years
   D) Probably in 11–20 or more years from now

---

40 Brinson, Singer, and Beebower, 'Determinants of Portfolio Performance II: An Update,' Finan-cial- Analysts Journal, May-June 1991

4. Over the next several years, you expect your annual income to:
   A) Stay about the same
   B) Grow moderately
   C) Grow substantially
   D) Decrease moderately
   E) Decrease substantially

5. Due to a general market correction, one of your investments loses 14 percent of its value a short time after you buy it. What do you do?
   A) Sell the investment so you will not have to worry if it continues to decline
   B) Hold on to it and wait for it to climb back up
   C) Buy more of the same investment...because at the current lower price, it looks even better than when you bought it

6. Which of these investing plans would you choose for your investment dollars?
   A) You would go for maximum diversity, dividing your portfolio among all available investments, including those ranging from highest return/greatest risk to lowest return/lowest risk
   B) You are concerned about too much diversification, so you would divide your portfolio between two investments with historically high rates of return and moderate risk
   C) You would put your investment dollars in the investment with the highest rate of return and most risk

7. Assuming you are investing in a stock mutual fund, which one do you choose?
   A) A fund of companies that may make significant technological advances that are still selling at their low initial offering price
   B) A fund that invests only in established, well-known companies that have potential for continued growth
   C) A fund devoted to highly diversified "blue chip" stocks that pay dividends

8. Assuming you are investing in only one bond, which bond do you choose?
   A) A high-yield (junk) bond that pays a higher interest rate than the other two bonds, but also gives you the least sense of security with regard to a possible default
   B) The bond of a well-established company that pays a rate of interest somewhere between the other two bonds
   C) A tax-free bond, since minimizing taxes is your primary investment objective

9. You expect inflation to return, and it has been suggested that you invest in 'hard' assets such as real estate and cable TV, which have historically outpaced inflation. Your only financial assets are long-term bonds. What do you do?

A) Ignore the advice and hold on to the bonds

B) Sell the bonds, putting half the proceeds in "hard" assets and the other half in money market funds

C) Sell the bonds and put all the proceeds in "hard" assets

D) Sell the bonds, put the proceeds in "hard" assets, and borrow additional money so you can buy even more "hard" assets

10. You have just reached the $10,000 plateau on a TV game show. Now you must choose between quitting with the $10,000 in hand or betting the entire $10,000 in one of three alternative scenarios. Which do you choose?

A) The $10,000—you take the money and run

B) A 50 percent chance of winning $50,000

C) A 20 percent chance of winning $75,000

D) A 5 percent chance of winning $100,000

Supporting Document for Chapter 5

Glossary of Terms

The following definitions of investment terms are from the US Securities and Exchange Commission's (SEC's) website at www.sec.gov.

Bonds

A bond is a debt security, similar to an IOU. When you purchase a bond, you are lending money to a government, municipality, corporation, federal agency, or other entity known as the issuer. In return for the loan, the issuer promises to pay you a specified rate of interest during the life of the bond and to repay the face value of the bond (the principal) when it "matures," or comes due. In contrast to bondholders who have IOUs from the issuer, shareholders are owners of the company they purchase.

There are many different kinds of bonds, including US government securities, municipal bonds, corporate bonds, mortgage and asset-backed securities, federal agency securities, and foreign government bonds.

The Securities Industry and Financial Markets Association has a website, investinginbonds.com, that contains basic information for investors about corporate and municipal bonds and useful tools for determining prices and yields for municipal and other bonds. The federal government also issues a variety of debt securities, including Treasury bills, notes, and bonds. For information about buying and selling Treasury securities, visit the website of the US Department of the Treasury's Bureau of the Public Debt.

Stock Funds

"Stock fund" and "equity fund" describe a type of investment company (mutual fund, closed-end fund, unit investment trust [UIT]) that invests primarily in stocks or "equities" (as contrasted with "bonds"). The types of stocks in which a stock fund will invest will depend upon the fund's investment objectives, policies, and strategies. For example, one stock fund may invest in mostly established, "blue chip" companies that pay regular dividends. Another stock fund may invest in newer, technology companies that pay no dividends but that may have more potential for growth. Another type of stock fund—an index fund—invests in stocks of companies contained in a particular market index. (There are also index funds that invest in bond indices.)

Like any investment, stock funds are subject to various investment risks. The prices of the stocks of companies in which the funds invest may fluctuate based on changes in the companies' financial condition and on overall market and economic conditions. This can affect the performance of a stock fund. Some stock funds attempt to minimize these risks by spreading out ("diversifying") their investments among different companies, industries, and markets. If a fund is diversified, its prospectus will tell you this.

Before investing in a stock fund, carefully read all of the fund's available information, including its prospectus and most recent shareholder report.

Mutual Funds

Disclaimer: Mutual funds are sold by prospectus only. Before investing, investors should carefully consider the investment objectives, risks, charges, and expenses of a mutual fund. The fund prospectus provides this and other important information. Please contact your representative or the Company to obtain a prospectus. Please read the prospectus carefully before investing or sending money.

A mutual fund is a type of investment company that pools money from many investors and invests the money in stocks, bonds, money-market instruments, other securities, or even cash. Here are some characteristics of mutual funds:

Investors purchase shares in the mutual fund from the fund itself, or through a broker for the fund, and cannot purchase the shares from other investors on a secondary market, such as the New York Stock Exchange or Nasdaq Stock Market. The price that investors pay for mutual fund shares is the fund's approximate net asset value (NAV) per share plus any fees the fund may charge at purchase, such as sales charges, also known as sales loads.

Mutual fund shares are "redeemable." This means that when mutual fund investors want to sell their fund shares, they sell them back to the fund, or to a broker acting for the fund, at their current NAV per share, minus any fees the fund may charge, such as deferred sales loads or redemption fees.

Mutual funds generally sell their shares on a continuous basis, although some funds will stop selling when, for example, they reach a certain level of assets under management.

The investment portfolios of mutual funds typically are managed by separate entities known as "investment advisers" that are registered with the SEC. In addition, mutual funds themselves are registered with the SEC and subject to SEC regulation.

There are many varieties of mutual funds, including index funds, stock funds, bond funds, and money market funds. Each may have a different investment objective and strategy and a different investment portfolio. Different mutual funds may also be subject to different risks, volatility, and fees and expenses. Fees reduce returns on fund investments and are an important factor that investors should consider when buying mutual fund shares.

Target-Date Funds

Recognizing this, a number of companies offer "target-date retirement funds," sometimes referred to as "target-date funds" or "lifecycle funds."

These funds are designed to make investing for retirement more convenient by automatically changing your investment mix or asset allocation over time. Asset allocation involves dividing an investment portfolio among different asset categories, such as stocks, bonds, and cash investments. Once you select a target-date fund, the managers of the fund make all the decisions about asset allocation.

Target-date funds are often available through 401(k) plans. Some 401(k) plans use these funds as the default investment for plan participants who have not selected their investments under the plan. Both before and after investing in a target-date fund, consider carefully whether the fund is right for you.

Target-date funds, which are often mutual funds, hold a mix of stocks, bonds, and other investments. Over time, the mix gradually shifts according to the fund's investment strategy. Target-date funds are designed to be long-term investments for individuals with particular retirement dates in mind. (Principal value is not guaranteed at the target date.) The name of the fund often refers to its target date. For example, you might see funds with names like "Portfolio 2030," "Retirement Fund 2030," or "Target 2030" that are designed for individuals who intend to retire in or near the year 2030.

However, target-date funds, even if they share the same target date—for example, 2030—may have very different investment strategies and risks. They do not guarantee that you will have sufficient retirement income at the target date, and you can lose money. Target-date funds do not eliminate the need for you to decide, before investing and from time to time thereafter, whether the fund fits your financial situation. Even if you plan to retire in 2030, you may decide, based on your investment objectives, tolerance for risk, and other assets, that a 2020, 2040, or other target-date fund is more appropriate for you. Or you may decide that you don't want to invest in a target-date fund.

Most target-date funds are designed so that the fund's mix of investments will automatically change in a way that is intended to become more conservative as you approach the target date. Typically, the funds shift over time from a mix with a lot of stock investments in the beginning to a mix weighted more toward bonds.

Money Market Funds

Disclaimer: An investment in the Money Market Fund is not insured or guaranteed by the Federal Deposit Insurance Corporation or any other government agency. Although the Fund seeks to preserve the value of your investment at $1.00 per share, it is possible to lose money by investing in the Fund.

A money market fund is a type of mutual fund that is required by law to invest in low-risk securities. These funds have relatively low risk compared to other mutual funds and pay dividends that generally reflect short-term interest rates. Unlike a "money market deposit account" at a bank, money market funds are not federally insured.

Money market funds typically invest in government securities, certificates of deposit, commercial paper of companies, or other highly liquid and low-risk securities. They attempt to keep their net asset value (NAV) at a constant $1.00

per share—only the yield goes up and down. But a money market's per-share NAV may fall below $1.00 if the investments perform poorly. While investor losses in money markets have been rare, they are possible.

An investor tendering mutual fund shares, including shares of money market funds, for redemption generally must be paid within seven days of tender. Pursuant to Section 22(e) of the Investment Company Act of 1940, registered open-end companies may not suspend the right of redemption and must pay redemption proceeds within seven days, except in certain emergencies or for such other periods as the Commission may by order permit for the protection of security holders of the company.

Before investing in a money market fund, carefully read all of the fund's available information, including its prospectus, or profile if the fund has one, and its most recent shareholder report.

Money market funds are regulated primarily under the Investment Company Act of 1940 and the rules adopted under that Act, particularly Rule 2a-7 under the Act.

Sustainable Investment Strategy™ "Baskets" Strategy
Sam and Sally Sample

Total Investable Assets Available
$1,603,000.00

Fixed Income		Equity Allocations			
Basket One	**Basket Two**	**Basket Three**	**Basket Four**	**Basket Five**	**Basket Six**
34%	7%	6%	6%	13%	34%
Years 1-5	Years 6-10	Years 11-15	Years 16-20	Years 21-25	Years 25+

		Moderate Portfolio of Investments	Balanced Portfolio of Investments	Aggressive Portfolio of Investments	Equity Aggressive Portfolio of Investments
Fixed Income Allocations		Liquidate at end of year 10	Liquidate at end of year 15	Liquidate at end of year 20	Liquidate at end of year 25

Target Allocations for Sustability

Cash / Money Market / CD	Fixed Annuity / Fixed Income				
$545,020	$112,210	$96,180	$96,180	$208,390	$545,020

Current Balances

Cash / Money Market / CD	Fixed Annuity / Fixed Income		
$200,000	$385,000	$630,000	$388,000

Action Required

Increase	$72,230	Decrease	$437,640	Increase	$365,410